Craigie's Clevedon Poems
(a novella with poems)

James Russell

NEWTON-LE-WILLOWS

Published in the United Kingdom in 2013
by The Knives Forks And Spoons Press,
122 Birley Street,
Newton-le-Willows,
Merseyside,
WA12 9UN.

ISBN 978-1-909443-02-0

Copyright © James Russell, 2013.

The right of James Russell to be identified as the author of this work has been asserted by him in accordance with the Copyrights, Designs and Patents act of 1988. All rights reserved. No part of this publication may be reproduced, stored in a retrieval system, transmitted in any form or by any means, electronic, photocopying, recording or otherwise, without prior permission of the publisher.

Acknowledgements:

Acknowledgements are due to the editors of the following magazines in which some of the poems first appeared: *Black Box Manifold, This Corner*.

For Carole

Editor's Introduction
by
Professor Elaine D. Palm
The Research Unit for the Study of Hermeneutics (Th.R.U.S.H.)
Department of Literary Epistemology
The University of Clevedon at North East Somerset

The text we have before us – the playfully anguished diary and the fifty or so poems of vertiginous variety – is not only problematic in its lazily ambitious range of concerns and cognitive contexts, but it is so insofar as the reader is adrift among its registers and rhetorics. Each prose passage is a decompression chamber between poems about which the reader wonders, to put it at its most mild and neuter, "What is their *status*?", "Where do I get my foothold?", "Where am I located *vis-à-vis* these outpourings?", "Am I witness to the unfortunate gropings of a sincerely striving amateur?", "Or am I *in loco* Mother Facey?" (The referent will be explicated, patient reader, in the text – as will this naïve confusion be dispersed in my piece!).

At the simplest, most literal and most banal, the text marks the dissolution of a 61-year-old second-division academic into a drink-sodden glutton. It is the mode by which a poet *manqué* expresses his literary prejudices and obsessions in the hope of finding what one may call 'a voice', or at least some epistemic orientation to the poetic. It is the account of a tragicomic love affair and subsequent tragicomic encounters. And it is a confession to a murder.

For those of you profoundly and naggingly exercised by this notion of *status*, one may put the matter boldly thus:

this Professor of Sociology has never published a poem in his life, he is sinking into alcoholism, he is in extremis, and the poems are often opaque by the standards of the marketplace, the out-of-town store, the Friday night bistro. Well, are they "any good"? Do they, it might be asked, "cut the mustard"? And, what's more, did their author *mean* them to be any good? Was he aiming to make art or aiming merely to get away with it? Well, as I am want to say to my Th.R.U.S.H. undergraduates, and yes even *post*-grads, and maybe even the odd post-doc (names in the same null class as pack-drills Claire dear, whoops!), those questions need unpacking, deconstructing, defusing, rendering defeasible, and problematicising. Now, one can hardly summarise a research programme in a few short sentences (Palm, 2000a, 2000b; Palm & Hodge, 2001a, 2001b; Palm, Hodge and Palm, 2002a, 2000b, 2002c; Palm, 2003a, 2003b; Palm, 2004; Palm, 2005a, 2005b; Palm and Hughes, 2006a; Palm and Hughes, 2007a, 2007b; Palm and Hughes, 2008; Palm, 2009 submitted; full references and PDFs at http//www/clevedon-litepist-thrush/palmoff.welcometome), but let me just say this: as to the first question I say "Good for *what*?", "Good for *whom*?", "Good according to *whose* conception of poetry and in *what* context?". And please do bear in mind the existence of – modesty is not holding me back at this juncture! – what I myself have coined as the *quantum theory of literary quality* (Palm, 2004), which means, in a quantum (!) nutshell, that we alter the, let's say, poem in the act of making a judgement on it. Then we have the second question, about whether the author was in any sense *aiming* for quality "in the first place". Well, why, in a frankly metaphysical sense, do we have to *care* about this? The words have found their way onto the page and we have a perfectly adequate neuroscientific story as to how that might have happened; while always bearing in mind that the brain sciences have once and for all rendered utterly jejune, and perhaps even nullified, the "very idea" of personal rather than sub-personal responsibility for our intentions; *We* "generate" intentions! That is the neuroscience of the stone-age and we literary theorists should at last "get real" about it; or, more soberly, "assimilate its lessons". Once again, I cannot do otherwise than reference my recently-made case for *neuro-criticism* in Palm (under review).

That said, I will, with some reluctance, return to the matter of 'motives' when I have set out some "facts of the case". One must "do one's duty" as editor "after all"!

John ('Jack') Craigie was born in Beckenham, Kent, on June 1st, 1946. To the surprise of many he gained an "Exhibition" to New College Oxford to study Philosophy, Politics, and Economics (PPE) in 1964. There he thrived in every domain, taking a First Class degree. After a Ph.D. at the London School of Economics, he took up a lectureship in Sociology at the University of Glasgow, later rising – *does* one rise in this regard? – to a Personal Chair in Social Theory. He was married three times, fathering three children with his first wife. He also had numerous brief affairs. Now, as my colleague Dr. Fran Clarke puts it, his life did indeed describe an arc – in the sense that it descended to earth at the last! But, at its high point, Craigie was an evangelical Marxist. As one of Craigie's oldest friends and sometime colleague Professor Peter Bovey puts it: "There was ever only one love in Jack's life and that was Karl Marx. Ironically, he got the Chair just as he was falling out of love. For the younger Jack, Marx could explain everything: from the nature of consciousness, to the state of the markets, to what's 'in' in the pop world. He even used to cultivate the look of 'the moor', for which his thick black hair came in handy; and there were the cigars in the London days of course. After that, after the Chair and the end of the life's love, he became an *agent provocateur*-cum-dandy, spending more time interrupting and monologuing at Philosophy, Psychology, and English seminars than in his home ones, though he was always there for drinks parties and the more contentious staff meetings."

So might there be a sense then – a throbbing gristle of sense or a wisp of intimation – that the author of this diary and these poems "turned to" literature after Marxian theory had "failed" him? For in the diary he shows himself to be well-informed (one means in, of course, the way of the rubber-necking outsider who is the bane of the professional theorist's life) about modern English verse and about the poetry scene. He had taken a considerable library of poetry on his travels. Some will ask what "lies behind" this. It has been said at least once that "Craigie is, above all, a wily man". So here – it has been "said", and I am here merely the conduit – that one workable narrative is that this poet *manqué* reasoned that his poems, maybe many of which had been written *before* the murder, might be folded into the diary of a murder, a text that would surely prove to be eminently *publishable*. In that way – and let us recall the description of Craigie too as being "opportunistic in the extreme" – something to his advantage would come about when he was eventually caught. Or might the narrative be instead that at the end of his tether he simply reverted to something he had always loved, in a quite private and, by his standards, sincere, way? It was the what-is-left-when-there-is-no-hope-and-I-am-covered-in-moral-dirt scenario.

But hark! Do I hear a rustle in the undergrowth? Do I hear the question posed seriously, by somebody over ten years old? The question I mean: is it not worth "knowing" which, if either, of these narratives is indeed "the case"? We at Th.R.U.S.H give an *enormous*, we give the sensory engulfment of an enormous, NO to this question. You have the *text* gentle reader, in its particularly masculine self-consciousness, its abject solipsism, and its ultimate feyness. Relax.

In addition to the AHRB, the ESRC, the WRBK, the YIWN, the TTFN, Clevedon City Council, *The Fruit-Face Juice Bar*, and *Gemima's Kitchen* I would like to thank my terrier of the touchpad, my rodent of the ring-file, my pug of the PowerPoint, little Dr. Claire Hughes for constructing the footnotes and writing the postscript in such a nice, concise way. Cheers Claire mate!

E.D.P.
Clevedon
November, 2009.

30th May, 2007

I look so strange to myself now. My first thought had been to go for a Little Richard look. Dye the hair to its original black, cut back and sweep upward my marvellously complicated locks to a pompadour, shave the goatee back to a pimp 'tache; and, of course, buy a big-shouldered suit, probably in light grey and certainly three sizes too big. 'Little Jack Craigie'. Not any more: 'Little *Duncan Poole*'. What were Richard's originally anal lyrics again?

> *Tootle Fruitie, Good Bootie*
> *If it don't fit, don't force it...*

And so in life...

But, I *was* forcing it, and even I could see so in that novel state I was in. I was too awake, those weeks ago. So waterlogged with energy I could drink down a half bottle of *Paddy*[1] as if it was *Tizer*.

Anyway, that style was only a kiss away from 'Flash Harry' who paraded in his velvet suit, with his white mane flying free, down Byers Road[2]. Though it is almost comforting to have one, I never did like that nickname. So unoriginal, and so far off the mark. It was disguise, not a display. And no, it is not remotely ironic that a disguise was exactly what I came to need, after I did that deed.

---

[1] A brand of Irish whiskey.

[2] A principal thoroughfare in the West End of Glasgow, near the University.

The best disguise, I soon came to realise, if I'm following me, was to have no mask, to strip the face and smooth it down. Be like the 21st Century male of the central tendency, the naked manikin in the box before you put on his wig and clobber and whiskers. The crash-test dummy, with crash-test mental states. I shaved off my hair and beard, found an old pair of spectacles as close as possible to National Health – Völkerspekula – and set about putting on weight. Six *Mars*[3] a day pumps the wrinkles away; with lashings of butter on the side; washed down with more lashings of Barley Wine. So now I'm beginning to look like a baby with responsibility issues. I'd aimed for something in the domain of Iain Sinclair[4], but ended up nearer Truman Capote, but Truman dressed in the M&S version of Gap. And in my beanie hat, so necessary now in the colder weather, I could be Benny Hill's brother released shell-shocked from the attic.

I do miss my *powerful* (© V. Nabokov and M. Amis) *Audi*, but cash in hand was what I had to have. I just don't want to think about what will happen when the money runs out. Pass myself off as an illegal immigrant, to shovel shit, or to pull pints in some dank pub. "Come on Bennyillchevikski, we wants servin' down 'ere. Look sharp, you fat tit." I'm going to bed.

---

[3] A popular confectionary of chocolate, caramel, and nougat.

[4] Psycho-geographer and friend of the English literary *avant garde*.

31st May, 2007

Two juicy problems. Number one. The big question was posed after breakfast (a wonderful grease-fest) by the not-so lovely landlady, Mrs Facey, about How Long I am Staying. "Well... a good few weeks at least." Raised eyebrows. "You see, this is just the kind of secluded spot I have been looking for to get some writing done." Writing. I found myself telling her I was a poet, for God's sake. I nearly said 'novelist'; but people expect to have heard of novelists. Nobody's heard of modern poets, except clapped-out academics such as I with too much time on their hands. Next problem. "Ooo lovely. Our Jason's a bit of a poet, so maybe he could..." So her gawk of a son will want to see my poems and show me his. Maybe the drooping one will try Googling 'Duncan Poole'. I had better say a "book-length piece is a new departure for me", that I've really only published in little magazines till now "but Faber have hinted at a contract..."

I'm going to bed with three *Mars* and the rest of the *Paddy*. Here's a poem for you Jason old son:

> *The dew is on the meadow*
> *And Glory does abound.*
> *I hear a maiden singing.*
> *Can you hear that fuckin' sound?*

1st June, 2007

Today is my birthday. That is all that needs saying on the matter, thank you Tony. Next please.

I am now 61. Oh ring dem bells! 61 = 'Inner Truth' in the I Ching. But, what I require, Mavis, is Outer Falsity.

What a dream about Nathan[5]. I just can't get it out of my head. Well, let it serve as the first Poem by the Poet Duncan Poole (henceforth: PPDP).

1. Neuroscience

Unimaginably cold, estranged, dishonest
Simple as a sock and meaningless:
Try it at home on a rainy Sunday,
Who shot John? on the record player.

For those with right real will and flair:
You can learn to remove your own head –
As from a prawn – at a certain tilt
A muddy click and then to hold the ball

Of your very self. A painless process,
Though pain floats up into
The brute poise of its return.
And after its return you duck like

---

[5] Craigie's only son.

A duck and swivel like a fan to check
That all's safe home. Do you believe me?
Do you? Huh? Perhaps there is a high
Empty shelf never dusted, a flimsy

Chair beneath the idea for a *roman
a clef*; despair in the bakery-hot
Thoroughfare, some shadow, some
Sorbet; this holiday for self help.

The mentioned fan surveys bitch patties
And black plans, a stiff neck, a letter
From my son Hannibal,
Recollecting the day of his sixth

Birthday and my tutorial in head
Removal. Palpable force
To settle his back home, pulp soft
But at an angle strained.

Clear fluid ran from his nose
And eyes. "I don't understand,
Dad" he said to me.

June 2nd, 2007

I left #1 in the Brother[6] so Mother Facey would find it when she comes snooping round. I imagine she called "Our Jace" up to witness the secretion. I can see them prodding it like a dead bird. Went for a walk along the front.

I was taken aback by the pier. I had imagined it would be decayed, broken-backed, rotten and rusted. Like a feeble charcoal sketch of something once beautiful. Like Bob Dylan. (No, really.) Something that looked elegantly frail from my window but was simple detritus close up. How wrong could I be. This was Bob Dylan who had been trained to sing amateur operetta, whose hair had been cut with a nice side-parting in the style of Kenneth.

> *Connor[7], who wore beige*
> *as befits a man of his age.*

The pier had been renovated, I think mainly by lottery money; and now every plank of its deck, every single one, had a little brass plaque in the style of "Mike, Avis, baby Neil and the Biggs family." Fine. But what was not fine was that the sides of the pier were just rows of boring planks, this time with 'in memoriam' and other heavinesses plaqued on them. Should they not be wrought iron? The main point here was to get the bugger open for

---

[6] This is a make of manual typewriter.

[7] Kenneth Connor was one of the *Carry On* team for many years. He had previously gained a limited fame as Sydney Mincing in Ted Ray's radio comedy *Ray's a Laugh*.

business, not to *restore* it in any sense. At the end was nothing. Where steamers used to set out for North Devon resorts was now, up a few steps, a counter selling croissants, cappuccinos, and speciality teas. This was a People's Pier, a bland promontory with a function. Walk along it, coffee, then back. It reminded me of the way young marrieds used to do up their houses in the early '60s – chopping off Edwardian exuberances, replacing newels with hardboard, fitting 'flush' doors.

The 'beach' by the pier is rock, pebbles, and seaweed, all tar-smeared – and mud, mud, mud. I walked out along the long-defunct stone jetty towards Wales (clearly visible factories), lifting up stones with a sucking sound, finding the occasional little grey crab. Then west along the Prom round a perky headland with a lovely wind-flattened tree and a bandstand. Down to the boating lake walled in from the sea – 'marine lake'. The miniature railway (*Rio Grande*) on the park called Salthouse Fields, the big cream pub sunk into the rocky woodland at the end of the further beach –*The Salthouse*. They all suit me just fine. The small scale, the perpetual Sunday feel, the impossibility of imagining a police car speeding past the bowling green and me in the back with a coat over me bleedin' 'ead. But they all force the thought of what I am going to do all day: eat *Mars* and chips, sit in the 'guest lounge', torture the Brother with smoke-screen poems?

But what about these here poems? I can produce objects that even quite educated people might mistake for poems. But I'd rather not have to do it. In fact, I don't think I really approve of poetry, at least of what it's become – that various thing. I like *poems*. It feels like, let's say,

Sunday Morning[8], *Wedding Wind*[9], *The Eolian Harp*[10] are my own little beetles in my own little boxes. I don't want to look at them too often in case their spell – not spell, quiddity, something like that – ever evaporates into the air. I certainly don't wish to memorise poems because I want them still strange enough to re-delight me.

But there is something corrupt about poetry now. I would rather read a well-knit sequence of sentences by Hugh Trevor Roper telling me about Henri IV and the Huguenots than open the shiny (and weirdly smelly) pages of *Poetry Review* for 14 lines of exquisite solipsism, no matter how much subtle artistry went into them. Or *is* it solipsism? No, it's more like all-in wrestling or circuit cycling. If you know the invisible guidelines, if you can see the nods and glances, they'll let you in and together you will all generate what civilians will see as something that is authentically what it advertises itself as being. Oddly though, I'm warming to so-called Late Modernism. In fact, *The Western Gate*[11] is one of my beetles. There's no eagerness-to-please, no fey pretension and there's

---

[8] A poem by the American poet and insurance man, Wallace Stevens

[9] A poem by Philip Larkin.

[10] This poem is one of the best-loved of Samuel Taylor Coleridge. Written on the 20th August, 1795, some six weeks before his marriage to Sara. He continued to re-work it as late as 1817. It is a fair supposition than it was written within yards of Nimrod House, in which Craigie was domiciled. While he would surely have known this fact, his diary makes no reference to it. Did Craigie make for Clevedon on some kind of Coleridgidean quest? See Professor Palm's introduction for a brilliantly radical rebuttal of the very idea of asking such a question. [Cheers Claire! Ed.]

[11] This is an early poem by (what the broadsheet press have called) the "Cambridge Marxist obscurantist" J. H. Prynne.

playfulness and linguistic sparking. It can be like a string of cross-word clues without solutions; but there is no actual code-cracking in the mainstream sense – no paraphrase, locked in the mind of some shell-shocked spinster of steely ambition: shell-shocked spinster and all-in wrestler. Maybe I'll start my own branch of Late Modernism – *The Don't Wait Up For Me, See You At Breakfast Clevedon School*, with my Facey acolytes.

I'll dip my toe some way in. Maybe one about the old dear who's just walked out of *Big Brother*.

2. Bye Just Now

Sanguine over too many leather hills,
brought to bear in summer, the silly matron
excuses her boredom like a fund-manager
his mosh-pit cavort. What the Dickens

to do now she is about to speak
seeing her celebrity homunculus in ruby
laudanum dregs. What's it to you shit
face the girls explain to her through

dreich. Zoom back from the house to vertigo
juncture, tell them the egg of circumstance
smashed freely about the career banshees.
We do not miss her cheeks and trench at all.

And some of the Late Mods are quite a larf. Gillian[12] dragged me off to a reading by a local guy called Peter Manson. Funniest thing I'd heard in years; though he was reading his prose *I think*. He runs a press called *Object Permanence*[13], which is supposed to be a nod to the invisible existence of the Scottish *avant garde*; though more likely he just liked the paratactic[14] heft of the noun phrase.

---

[12] Professor Gillian Browne-Smythe from the English Faculty at Glasgow, a friend of Craigie.

[13] A term coined by the polymath and Swiss Jean Piaget. It refers to babies' ability to search for rattles behind cushions when they cannot see them at all.

[14] Parataxis is abutting syntactic elements rather than having them in a subordinating relationship ("the permanence of objects"), employed much by Ezra Pound and much more by J. H. Prynne, on whom see footnote 11.

James Russell

3. Object Permanence or The Perduring Existence of the Scottish *Avant-Garde* despite its Lack of Visibility[15]

Chick Murray and Maidie[16]
Chick Murray and Maidie
Chick Murray and Maidie
Chick Murray and Maidie
Chick Murray and Maidie
Chick Murray and Maidie
Chick Murray and Maidie
Chick Murray and Maidie
Chick Murray and Maidie
Chick Murray and Maidie
conjure innocence from
Chick Murray and Maidie
Chick Murray and Maidie
Chick Murray and Maidie
Chick Maidie and Murray
Murray Maidie and Chick
And Chick Maidie Murray
Chick plus (IPA=) Medi
Chick bacillus shunt for

---

[15] Some of the words were done with pen and ink in this poem. Craigie obviously took a lot of care over it.

[16] Scottish entertainers of the old school. Not Late Modernists. They divorced before Chic died, but remained close.

Maidie now temper-evident trys
macquette option sin convert
on vitrification of "sad shit"
to buck the line vector &

lie as if helium balding 0.096%
for takers evid
ent
no please and Chick to sigh rear-guardéd
fuck-face   she 4 feet 11 inches tall accordionist
Chick wife freebasting nose-guard assail from
Chick Maidie and Murray
Chick Murray and Maidie
Chick Murray and Maidie
Chick Murray and Maidie
Chick Murray and Maidie

Chick speaks: "So anyway – I told him, didn't I, Maidie? – well I couldn't ignore the fella could I? There he was. I could see him. I couldn't help but see him because he was there."

I enjoyed that. I feel better. I'm off out for a new bottle of *Paddy*. Only 4 Mars today.
I'll be wasting away.

6th June, 2007

The off-licences were all closed, so I went to *Campbell's Landing* (pub by the pier) and bought a bottle of *Teachers* (liquid pepper with cat-pee after-notes) at some great cost, staying on to down five pints of *Courage Best* with *Jack Daniels* chasers, and playing the juke box. I was *glowing* when I walked up Copse Road to Nimrod House – you could of fried an egg on me 'ead. I was ready for intelligent conversation, then loud rock on my Walkman.

Old Shine[17] was in the lounge, watching *Newsnight*. Shine is intelligent and his conversation is un-abating, so in I went. He's Jewish-disputatious, and has the way of not letting you finish a sentence if he thinks it will pull the matter away from him. He does it by pretending he didn't hear your first phrase, cupping his hand to his ear and saying 'Eh' – *yes really that is really how he does it*. Stone me. I say, stone me. He wears the other down. I began making comments about Paxman's guests, then about Paxo's now-grey hair and his expression of mock shock ("Not shock jock but mock shock", I jested). He glanced at his watch, turned to me: "Wordsworth and Shelley were tea-total." "But I'm not a Romantic," I slurred. "What the hell are you then!" "I'm one of the cowboy poets." I felt a despairing euphoria. "We only drink alcohol and only eat Pontefract Cakes. Yup, I sure am." I saw Shine was about to get up, but would not be left. I beat him to it. "Well, ah guess ah better mosey on

---

[17] Philip Shine, a retired accountant from London, holidaying in the South West.

up the wooden hill and write down anotheruh ma pomes, afore gittin' some shut-eye."

Climbing the stairs I turned back and patted the *Teachers* bottle at Shine. "Or mebee I'll jess sit up with ma sick friend."

I didn't sit up. I drank up, and danced up and down the room in my headphones. I must have been singing along with Little Richard; and my step is no longer light. I recall a knocking on the door and something about "Mr Pool... Duncan... you all right?" in a woman's voice.

The next day and the one after that I spent in bed being buggered senseless by reality. Mother Facey impressed me. She never once came up to ask diplomatically if I was ill. I can just see Shine sharing his impressions with other guests.

I thought I had better have something to show for my absence so I left #4 and #5 on my desk. When I'm in my little cell I can only think about people. The Don't-Wait-Up-for-Me schtick requires abstraction and objectivity and some kind of zest. I thought about what Sabbine[18] must now be doing in the evenings; I thought too about poor 'Jace' and that he might be flattered to have a poem about himself.

---

[18] Sabbine Stripentau, Craigie's lover, and the mother of Nobby.

4. Night Fever

The kids all in bed, and Parky's on
Not abandoned but passed.
Loose at the far end
of a long settee,
photographs, 'slim-n-sexy'
hungry, gnawing
at the facts of him
like a Bugatti gnaws
at a labyrinth of corners.
She
acquaplanes
into black.

5. About Facey

I. Facey and art history

There was not a young man called Dalí
There was not a young man called Buñuel.
But there was a young lady who
Lived in a chalet
Who knew Jason Facey very very well.
She got to know him too well.
For later she saw that there's no man called 'Facey'
Of the extension which
From that proper name fell.
Now each has gone his and her own way,
Each down a Peterborough-brick-built alley -
Neither designed by I. K. Brunel.
Their slit eyes ooze liquid from this taking of leave.
Oh Dog Oh Dog please grant him *joie de vivre*.

II. Facey and the music business

'There's mother again tapping at the window
Her little eyes alight with mischief.
Now what's that – dear God – in her mouth!'

Sitting inside his suit, a pie in its crust,
He would shift and twitch
And simmer speaking upwards into air.

"Still, she's come on pre-tty bloo-dy well
Since her operation. Full of vim.
Chock full of the stuff."

Facey had been telling me about his latest project:
Iconoclasts for Fourth Estate.
The argument of Chapter Six – Billy J. Kramer –

Oozed from him like ectoplasm.
"He could withstand as t'were
The Tyranny of the Beatle Cut.

"He could have passed for a Kennedy brother.
You'd say his clothes were bandbox fresh
Had he been a chick.

"And you should see him now.
Fearsome dear boy, a beach-bum
Psychopath. That Gorgon stare.

"One imagines him drawling answers
To the commission: "Hobbies? lemme see
Drunk drivin', life-threatnin' sexual practices."

'He lived – as do I d'you see –
In what I like to call The Weather
Of the Giant's Thumb.'

As ever, Facey's monologue
Drove into the self-referential sand.
He turned the music up; I sidled out

To explore the estuary. An hour
It must have taken me to cross it
Reciting to my panting self:

"Facey, Facey, oh Facey!
You used to have nose for shit
And now you have a taste for it.

You've not moved on my manky hero
Since you wanked under bedclothes
To Helen Shapiro."

Fathers call this 'the best part of the day'.
And here was Facey's mother stumbling gently
And with muddy slippers

Up to me, cup of tea in hand
(Needless to say stone-cold).
I told her that she needn't have

She said:
"I wanted an excuse to breathe the air
 Of this sky bleeding light into brusèd clouds, to taste

The symphonic freedom of the estuary,
Symbolising the exhaustion of all hope
And the birth of it. Biscuit?"

III. Facey takes some drugs

Such an awakening.
Here he was with a
Head pushed chinwards by a waterfall
Of hard fact.
Breathing was a challenge,
An alien tongue and
Trophied in his nose –
Bronze-age arrow-heads of bogies.
Consciousness was intolerable, as was the bed.
The breakfast caff was intolerable and offered no escape.
As the door to the outside world said 'Closed'.
Decision: more drugs.

A little later he was planning a party
And it was to be the first party of the 21st century.
He would paint a pointless word
Upon his forehead
And spray the window-panes silver.
He'd invite the famous La Bulosé
Rumoured to be the love child of
'Boy' St. Clare and 'Baby' Hertfordshire
Who would perform her party trick -
Cabbage whites flying from the parts
Of her now best dubbed 'public'.
He would impress and astonish all
By being other than he was.
The party would continue in New York for
Three further weeks.

IV. Facey goes into politics

Brave brave Jason Facey!
A mountain climbed
A dragon slain.
Big boy, bigger growing,
His white suit always bravely showing
Each new piss stain.

V. Facey as a dog

He had a mistress who walked beside the sea.
There was a minor mountain in the sea.
The sea was its old disinterested self
Not troubling the landscape with its solopsistic waves.

The minor mountain suggested Gormengast and Elgar's First.
It was in swimming distance – but not for Facey.
Some people thought the whole thing good as television:
Something where nothing is lost by an in-car view.

Facey jumped about the swish of foam
As if it were the fringe of a raped township
And what was out there was a doggy version
Of our dry familiar streets.
She slipped his lead and urged him go
And gazed indifferently out to sea.
The sea-birds didn't taunt him,
But Facey thought they fuckin' did.

Running into the sea as they flitted out of reach
Like schoolgirls, he thought they called to him
"Can't catch us dopey!". In fact, they'd cried
"Öd und leer das Meer."

Some holidaymakers loved Facey
For downwards of two minutes
Grinning into their kagouls:
"Guess what that symbolises, Corinne?"

Sweet Facey, the sandy dog, too self-absorbed
For tragedy, too small and ragged for the romantic turn,
Too dog for human too human for a dog.
Sweet Facey, the sandy dog, charging out to sea
As if Nature were reversible, as if
Another set of facts obtained,
Waiting for sea-birds to fly
To him like the little mountains.

You really can't beat the old favourites: chopped up prose plus hazy surrealism. But I would like to hear the Facey one shouted through a megaphone in a broad Brummie accent.

8th June, 2007

Terry Hall[19] has died, so I read. I love the obituary columns, my favourite bit of the paper. You get to see what lay behind-the-scenes those years ago. That the twinkly-eyed actor from Children's TV, the one who always played magicians and kindly uncles in on the kids' secret, was a crypto-fascist who lived with a South African dentist called Nigel. *Got the idea!*

I'm old, or oldish, now and know there was never anything behind my scenes. I ended up looking like Billy Connelly's mini-me complete with a 'what's next?' grin, well-liked in the Adam Smith[20] coffee room, being loquacious and absolutely no threat. I was no threat because for as long as I can remember I have simply told people what was upfront in my consciousness, and this was either sheer silliness or a list of things I had failed to bring off; but all recounted with a smile. I fell short, years ago when it came to taking the big leap of faith. I didn't take it. And there I was, a man of some distinction 'risen without trace'[21] as a purveyor of the soggiest grade of social anthropology. I have never aimed to impress. Old

---

[19] This is not the vocalist from *The Specials, Fun Boy Three, and Colour Field* – the early supporter of Bananarama. It is a ventriloquist who appeared on television in the late '50s and early '60s. His puppet was Lenny the Lion, an effete, lisping, benign creation. On the former see my 'Rock Against Racism: Hall, Bragg and Steele, three artists in tension'. *Semiotics Review*, (2004) Volume 2, pp 65-87.

[20] The Adam Smith Building is the social science building of Glasgow University.

[21] This phrase is attributed to Kitty Muggeridge, the wife of Malcolm, who was a public intellectual. Sir David Frost was the referent.

Figgis[22] once said to me that I looked like somebody who was all persona, like a cross between Velasquez and a clown, happiest when on display; but that really I had no persona at all. "You're Hume's man, Jack. No more than a bundle of desires and impressions, all mulched up with words. Most of us are like the facades of merchant banks, and you're a hardware store spilling onto the street."

It's been ages since I published anything; and lately I have been just going around being clever. I encouraged my younger colleagues *not* to publish. "We've got to put food on the table, Jack." Or they thought I was joking. Do I look ironic? No, they thought that my nature was exhausted by what I said: nothing behind it you see. "You see!" I'm sounding like Archie bloody Rice now. Anyway, my life was a Mardi Gras parade of ambiguous affairs in which I behaved like a shit or a six-year-old. "That's Jack for you," they'd say. And culminating in *this*. No comedy this time.

I knew Sabbine did not suit me. But boy did she take me seriously. Women often do – *did*. With her I felt a weight behind my words, a generative core. *Oh shut up!!* She made me feel like a star. A star! People call you a star now if you have a light for their fag or an inch of milk for their coffee. Terry Hall was a star. He deserves a tribute, with my special Don't Wait Up For Me sauce poured over it.

---

[22] A colleague, Juan Figgis.

6. Terry Hall (1926-2007)

Perfect heart, then stain-driven, all this way
down, far down to zombie judgement:
"I have a pain" is no statement surely
while cream and shandy pour from cracks
be calm all these canals crossed North
to South, glimpsed from loft vehicles.

Shining heat, shattered like confectionary
while all about think of you as a phone card.
If it's a rotten bridge pass quick and light,
'cus frankly these emotions are as earth
boiling in a window-box, may wreck
a hairdo or crust skin, but – be reverent

Terry – the distance renders safe.
This is not the gilded gallows of the chemical
philosopher: it's a hows in a nise streat. Lenny!
You are not forceful enough to keep a boat
in Chichester harbour, despite your eyes the eyes
of a sheep-killing dog, a face stone above that
line of trees seasick green, loosing your happy
heart upon us. Oh, you embawess me.

10th June, 2007

I've made some new friends from among the Nimrod inmates – Dave and Trish Bigwood. Dave greets me each day: "All right, Dunc?"

Dave's a minotaur, shoulders like an overstuffed sofa, laser-blue eyes, mid-50s, grey hair swept back curling up over his collar like what's-his-face Greene of *Top Shop*. Be-suited. Looks formidable. And then the poor sod speaks. Not so much Bristolian as sit-com Bristolian, and high and excited like a 7-year-old of indeterminate sex on Christmas morning. I'd love to hear him say in a Louisiana accent "Today's mah name-day and we're all goin' to church, and when we come home we're gonna have roast chickin with garden-grown peas; and paw's gonna drink some sherry wine." Trish is sexy, thin, been around but learned nothing so far as I can see, except surely some lewd expertise. Draws life from Dave. Her eyes suck some necessary juice from his smiling beefy face as it squeaks on about food and his childhood memories. She's not Bristolian: indeterminate accent, clipped delivery like a high-class receptionist.

Dave was rhapsodizing today at breakfast, telling Trish about trips he's had to Clevedon with his mum and dad ("arr muh and daad"). He explains, as if he is a palimpsestiste in the Sinclair mould, that the coffee bar on the front used to be a Fortes ("Forteyz") ice-cream parlour. Oh good God the Knickerbocker Glories ("Gloreyz") he's enjoyed there. And don't start him on the pier. One evening "arr daad and arr muh" drove down from Bristol in the motorbike-and-side-car (Dave within). In those days

– see – there was a mini amusements-arcade and a jukebox at the end. He heard Don Gibson singing *Sea of Heartbreak*, and on the way home they had stopped at a chippie. Young David had had steak-and-kidney pie and chips. The evening air, the song playing as the distant lights of Wales twinkled, then later the pie innards flooding the vinegary chips. The 'old man' had been in a jolly mood for once.

Trish was riveted, so much so that she seemed teetering on the threshold of outright shock, a novel kind of Trish-shock with a continuous aspect. If he'd told her he had gone for a swim she would have exploded. Well... I'm ashamed to say they remind me of Sabbine and me in the early days: past meals and pointless boy-hood episodes can be my stock-in-trade when I'm happy; and poor Dave is soppy-happy. Then, like me, he will break into song...

The loits in the 'arberr
Doan shoyne fur me

Then... oh dear...

lost love and loneliness,
memories of your caress

...weirdly, without the accent. I came upstairs and wrote PPDP number 7. Memories of our first caresses. A whole weekend in bed, my green sheets, not eating, hardly even

7. Nourishment

"What shall we talk about now?" your eyes
to mine and mine to yours in green
sheets your green eyes millennia ago

Later these were our skeletons stock still
locked in the pallet of a kiss
articulately leaning each to the other

We had no wish to eat but surfed
instead the tides of thought washing
through our eyes. And now blue-jays

cache in our balanced loins
while there's fecundity in the air, lifts
molecules from our bones and into

the lungs of lovers, unconfident maybe
in a winter of spring weather each says,
he says "I'll hold you to 'for ever'"

drinking. Actually, not that much sex. Talking, drinking in each other's faces – actually getting to know each other, like two strangers; but doing so in bed.

It's strange how I spent so long over number 7. Maybe not so strange that it ended up weak and sentimental. I typed and retyped it just to change a word, as if that could squeeze some art into it. Why? When it could have been done by one of the Liverpool Boys – maybe Craig Charles[23] on an off day? It has the mark of a Liverpuddle doesn't it? That is, poetic *thoughts* – or their idea of poetic thoughts (= sophomore surrealism plus closing-time pathos, utter *softness*) – expressed in flat unpoetic language. It's a way of *lying*. Actually, the weekend was dull. She was first silent, watching me as if for a false move, and then wittering. I was glad when she left. (*No, I wasn't. At least you can tell the truth to yourself, Jack.*)

But why am going on in this *Daily Mail* mode? Why am I taking this all so *seriously*? To keep the Faceys happy, I might just as well have plagiarized some of the recent products of Salt[24], or some other House of the Rising Sons of JHP. I might have spliced a bit of John Williamson into a bit of Drew Milne, and who would have ever noticed!? Better, I could have alternated lines. If every modernist poet from Bath to Penzance had paraded past my typewriter not one of them would have spotted the fraud.

Went for an après-lunch (= large chips with curry sauce and three *Mars*) drink in *Campbell's Landing*. It's been so rainy here I had to wear my beanie variety hat. The pub was almost uninhabited when I walked in. A gaggle of builder types was at the bar. They looked up at me, still briefly in my hat. One of them (the oldest one, as fat as I aspire to be) said something to his mates that fired a

---

[23] Irrepressible comic Craig would sometimes read one of his poems when contributing to Ned Sherrin's *Loose Ends*. This was when it was broadcast on Saturday morning. He is now a soap actor and DJ.

[24] Then a major publisher of The Cambridge School (of late modernist verse). Professor John Kinsella may have had a hand in naming it *Salt*.

laugh then settled to a rolling snigger as they watched me order a pint and take it to a table. He, who was probably the foreman/charge-hand, seemed to be coaching them in something. He was. They broke into song...

Billy Bean[25] built a machine
To see what it would do

The rest was dum-dah-dees then these two lines repeated ad lib, glancing over their dusty shoulders at me, who was pretending to be engrossed in a *Clevedon Mercury* found on the chair beside me. I went up for a second pint, before I was ready for one, out of what felt like bravado. "Yer Frank. 'es 'ordrin' another beanie-pint... 'es takin' it back to 'is beanie-seat... Yer! 'Es startin' to read 'is beanie-paper again. 'ows about that?" This was the youngest of the group sucking up. They all thought it was bloody hilarious. I headed for the gents. Now if this had been the USA, I calmly thought, one of them would follow me in and flush my head in the 'john'. But no – praise the Lord! – it's the UK, so another said in a deep Welsh voice "Oooo, look lads. He's going for a beanie-slash." I ordered a third pint, *Smiles* this time ("What, no beanie-crisps!?") and sat back down.

I could easily have left. After all, this was the one thing they did not want. What I really wanted to do was to confront them. But I have never mastered icy contempt and

---

[25] Bean was a character on BBC children's television in the 1950s. He had a sidekick called Yoo Hoo who was a dopey cuckoo, much given to egg-laying. This was the theme-tune.

would have ended up cussing and calling them dolts or oafs or retards or oiks or *abortions* or something hysterical like "nasty pieces of furniture." I couldn't take the chance of them kicking off. They must have been at least on their fifth pints. And what if the barman called the coppers? Curtains for me.

Then Big Dave Bigwood walked in. My first thought was whether he'd spotted my 'discomfiture'. "Dunc!!!" Then he saw the beanie-boys and his grin widened. "What are you doin' 'ere you useless little cunts!" He put the foreman into a headlock till his face was at bursting point. "Phone 'is mum," he said. "Tell 'er I got 'im, and I'm bringin' 'im 'ome for 'is tea."

They worked for Dave, it turned out, and had just finished a job up the road. Dave beckoned me over. He introduced me as his 'mate' as I watched *their* 'discomfiture' – much simpering. "You wanna watch ol' Dunc," he said, "'cus 'e might write a poem about you. Summat like...

> *Oh who are they all drinkin' Fosters?*
> *I will tell yew:*
> *Bigwood's tossers"*

I made my excuses and left.

14th June, 2007

I've been growing bored with the *Paddy*+reading+radio and have been spending the evenings in pubs – the bigger, and therefore the more anonymous, the better. Last night I was in one near the Triangle. It was like a work's canteen but with exhausted leather sofas dotted about it and enormous, low tables. In the corner of one of these sofas I chased *Budovar* and *Jack Daniel's* and watched most of *Titanic* (subtitled). My sofa backed on to one on which two old gays were chatting. I have bat ears so I could pick up the complaint from one of them that the ointment he now had to apply for an anal fissure could not be combined with Viagra. "So it's praying at the alter for me for the next eight weeks, love. I mean... I *ask* you!"

I sat and drank and watched Kate Winslett emote, and shuddered at what I was hearing. Kate seemed to shudder too as the guy carefully articulated 'a-nal *fiss-ure*'. I'm sure I heard the ghost of Tony Hancock whisper "Stone me, what a life."

The summer has been so wet. Water outside and water inside. The lovebirds were running down pale corridors as the sea gushed under doors. Didn't Freud take water to symbolise emotion? I had tears in my eyes by the end, not for Winslett and diCaprio but for me – *The Titanic*. Somewhere in my sub-person I was reasoning like this. Because I'm insubstantial, I will always float on the surface of emotion. I never miss people, I don't know what nostalgia is, I don't fall in love (though I say 'I love you' about as easily as 'ice and lemon?'). But I've been *holed*. I feel *guilt*. It's an emotion at its heart and it has emotion-blood pumping around it. And yes, it's a self-sentence too: "You're a sinner and you will pay for your sins." The self-sentence fuels the emotion. It's not actually the murder I did: it's the use – the *use* – I made of Sabbine, sailing across the Pacific of her love for me. Sabbine as an amenity. Did I not care about how it was with her because I'm 'insubstantial'? No, because I'm selfish and content to do bad things. This did not bother me, until now.

Her mind was on me all the time. Walking home down the hill I thought of the drawing neurologists present to stroke patients to test for language deficits – 'The Cookie Jar'. The patients have to describe what's going on in it. A woman is drying-up, staring out of the window in a daydream, 1940s-wide skirt, long perm, while a torrent of water overflows from the sink ignored onto the floor. In the background, her two children (I say 'her', as she's clearly middle class, no hired help) are toppling from a high stool they're using to reach 'the cookie jar'.

Sabbine more or less ignored her kids. She lived for men – for the *love* of men. And yet she trained the children – it surely was training, wasn't it? – endlessly to say "I love you, Mummy." The older ones would as often say "Ich liebe dich, Mutti". I can't go into this now. It's too bad. Some other time.

Shine cornered me about Tony Blair's resignation when I got back. I did number 8 this morning.

8. The Cookie Jar

The tiny ones as kitchen eels, pin-toothed, shim-
tight: "We love you, Mummy/Bunny/Meter
reader. Four snackies each is never enough." Miles

away she's at the sink, her charm-school stance
framed for the ravening man in mind, his cold
subversive passion torrents from sink to floor

in a garden path. Cord blood and love lie
about the house in shining pools
& she serene as kiddies topple now from stools.

She knows their quaint greeds, knows frame-
freeze before chasm, that "see" leads to "know" but
not always to "speak"; not for those

who have become their own initials in textbook
indexes, famous for their little chasms: the Wernikes
as talent-free late modernists, Brocas topple across

the torrents from open-class word to open-class
word & then the indefinables with their defuse
insults or even the normally-gagged-with-wine

& fear staring hard at the turning events
thinking 'it serves them right' and saying
on a good day a simple "Oh boy! Oh boy!"

16th June, 2007

There are actually days when I feel happy in this life. I've grown attached to the way the walls of *Mars Bars* collapse in sheets – in plates – and the innards of the bar are raggedly revealed with caramel fangs biting down onto the silt. And I've long dreamed of a life in which I could sip *Paddy* and watch the sunset knowing I had absolutely nothing to do the next day. But most of all there is the joy of being on holiday from oneself. (I love the way Poole is so much *slower* than Craigie.) Not that it was much of a self of course. Let's say a holiday from that walled round, propped up agglomeration of mental flotsam.

But there is a But. There is nobody to talk to now. I don't mean – I don't *want* – companionship. I want talk. What am I when I am non-verbal? A big lecture was the apotheosis of Jack Craigie. Even the poems are a form of talk to the Facey-interface. I remember Gillian[26] telling me – she had 'looked me up' – that Jack Craigie is who he is because I not only have the Sun in Gemini, but also the Moon and Mercury, and that she would 'bet good money' I had a Gemini Ascendant too. She 'warned' me I had Scorpio in Mars and in Venus though. What bollocks! One dirty old tramp says to another on a park bench "What sign were you born under, then,Ted?" "Faeces." (Thank yew ver much ladeezangents. Don't forget: I'm here till Friday.)

---

[26] Gillian [pronounced with hard 'g' as in 'good', in the Scottish manner] Paul, a friend of Craigie, and a New Age enthusiast.

I can talk to Shine, but he is not interested in listening to anybody. He is impatient, an egoist through and through. He seems to think that all these alt-Europa Jewish tics (the shrug, eyes and palms heavenwards, the tick-tock head, the camply beseeching lift of the voice at the end of a sentence, the mechanical irony) presents a kind of human warmth, welcoming the listener to the hearth... "Engage with me, already". But it's no more welcoming to me than a nose-pick or a stutter. And what an opinionated old sod he is. And the bit of learning he has, worn as lightly as horse-armour.

But there is always Jason. I've given him all the PPDPs now. But I'm sure he'd seen them all already via his mum. I expect Mother Facey stands guard as he reads them. I bet she whooped with joy as if he'd just got a place at Oxford when she saw 'About Facey' on the Brother.

I invited the lad in for a drink yesterday. *Paddy* and Coke for him. He's been giving me what passes for conspiratorial looks ever since 'About Facey'. Actually, I like our Jace. I generally like 18 year olds. Undergraduates are at their best in their first year. He does look odd though. He's not that tall by today's standards (about 6 foot maybe) but everything about him is long – face, arms, legs, neck, even his ears. His body is a mere origin of extremities. The voice is deep but always seems to be threatening to shatter like flawed bakelite.

He was so nervous. Maybe the shaven head suggested 'gay' to him. After one drink he started to relax, so much so that he asked if I would be good enough to 'cast my eye' over some of his 'verses'. Delighted! I was bracing myself for his asking me to 'explain' mine; but thank God he did not. Then he became weirdly bold after a couple of drinks and asked if I knew whether Ashbery [27] was "possibly homosexual, by any chance?" No, most *certainly* not I told him. He is a grandfather four times over. His wife ('Granny Ash') shuns the limelight. Her name is Irma – a Polish lady. I also told him Ashbery had had affairs with Ayn Rand and Margaret Mead in the 1950s and a torrid fling with Sophie Tucker resulting in a love child, a girl they named 'Mama'. Why did I do that? Because, while liking our Jace as I do, that question, and a few other things he said, told me that he was not so much a poetry lover (a creepy enough phrase in itself) but a poetry *groupie*. It's poets that interest him, not poetry. He likes the whole idea of 'a poet' and would very much like to turn into one, with writing some of the stuff a means to that end.

Did he detect a piss-take? Maybe, because he immediately became a bit chippy, chippy enough to ask whether I was "running away from the possibility of finding a poetic voice." He clearly impressed himself by that remark. Why was I such a "chameleon" he pressed. I dead-batted. A *voice* is something you have or you don't have. "Trying to develop one is a sad enterprise," I rather sadly said.

I felt in the end I had to placate him, so I agreed to come to his 6th Form English Society to give a reading.

Why???

---

[27] This will be John Ashbery, Pulitzer-Prize-winner and co-founder of the 'New York School' of poets.

But he seems to have pushed me into a run of three –
three, count 'em! – Don't Wait Ups.

9. Diana Talk

Unable to get away
        with a brief sentence,
to announce her support for some
        view of witchcraft;
I would like to rectify the baffling
in human behaviour from my alpha cottage.
Read with care, reveals her imbecility
turning into a whole literary genre,
nasty about people

        who are kind. A woman with a face
like a bird remains divided
as to the serious settlements, told me
father-as-boss (that historian of consumption)
        told me the age of the modern
        museum was dawning. I took the steep
stair not the concealed lift, committed
        neither 'looting' nor 'rape'
deserved to be remembered as more
than the cause of her unhappy life: incoherent
        as history, coherent as tract. Publish

the report about the summer storm,
the lightening, Mexico, about her new-found passion
        for the shit-stirrer. Some summer this
almost with words only for company slit
        to help me release dirty linen

like a party-pooper from the Alma Tunnel,
wanting only innocent pleasure with my Most
    Affectionate Lovinge Soveraine
and getting this cream or ream of days, the text
half the length of the old, a photo-journal, more
referred to than read. This
   is
    it: a simple arrangement
of five dots known
as a 'glider' or sometimes as
Dog Violet.

10. Sand Bar Flies

In my sleep I was kissing someone's
lips – one of my she-enemies
rendered soft by flattery and Guinness.

We had done with interest rates
and grain sales. Passion welled like
a sneeze; but I spend only 'the blood

of idols', the work of my fingers far
from fruition: the doe-girl undefiled
no balm for her in the villages, her

earrings ripped from her head; to her
I said "I will go out as before, and shake
myself, present to you my grit-smeared

sceptre." Patinir-blue through the window-
plants, one cloud like a case of vodka
left outside the door. If I am

a Man of Glory, then she is
my dream diviner. If I am a life-
guard with a leaden arm

then she is my Loves' Encampment.
This world of jocks and cookie
pushers, of moisturising men;

these deserted souls will be as to
the clever-as-ever baby charmers
as a sherry-bulge when
we wake together in the hot sand.

11. The World of Tim Frazer

Make a list
Make a fist
Make a wish
for little boxes for cufflinks, hearing-aids
to yield their sortal names up to you
snapping indestructibly shut, quilted those
things to which you swim
        with dead hands. You

advance an argument about
liquidity like a sharp-pronged buck;
yet all is still and coolly moving
the carpet in the pretty home
counties, some mystery, some
        cardigan; all

        are jungle-brained bar Tim
expects nothing & then a cupboard
affords a fright to him.

Stand back Tim to the best
boy or the camera pusher. See

        Tupper from the petrol station is
a forest fire of circumstance for all
to endure with the sexually active people
in the village. They rut & rent

        stand smoking and smirking on the
green, harass by advent, extend from the bush-
        green cars. Tim

unbuttons his cardigan, mumbles into mouthpiece
stretches out to the Mike Sammes Singers
considers how radio producers like to broadcast
their 10 year olds' depressive diaries.

20th June, 2007

Well, they just won't do will they!? Poor man's Ashbery plus a hint of cut-up, plus hope-for–the best. Inspiration? 9 = the recent swell of Diana talk (10 years since her death, I think), with books, birthday concert etc., flogging a dead princess; 10 = a dream of kissing a *bête noire* colleague and thoughts of drinking with her in happier days; 11 = reading something about Francis Durbridge[28]. Hardly late modernism, is it? More cooling your heels in reception two hours early. What they lack above all is conviction, call it commitment, call it *quality*. A toe in the water, playing at being playful. Though if I read them quickly and try to forget I wrote them they're not too bad. 11 has a certain swing to it.

Look, I think I'll go the whole hog and try to write some definitely Prynnish ones[29]. Where good poetry is wine, Prynne is one of those super-strong malt whiskeys that can't be drunk undiluted, so peaty it's a drink other than whiskey, whose purpose is to purge your system. Of what? Linguistic habits? Defunct ideas about how language relates to reality, and about its limits? The idea seems to be to strip the fur of cliché from your tongue. No, not cliché: the silting-up by a language without force, a fleecey language that muffles cognitive energy. Am I making myself clear? Of course you're bleedin' not. You have nothing there to be clear about. You are grinding out more cliché.

---

[28] Comfortably bourgeois thriller-writer, often televised in the late '50s/early '60s...

[29] In the style of Jeremy Prynne. See footnote 11.

And why am I writing like this? One may more truly say Prynne is a "glass of pure water" (MacDiarmid[30]). And why am I bothering at all? All I'm doing with these poems of mine is shoring up a cover story and passing the time. I'm like a dog worrying a raisin.

Enough of these watery thoughts, for today has been a good day and needs to be chronicled. During the day Clevedon rose to gorgeousness on the back of the weather, while in the evening a chance television view showed me how to deal with this bloody 6th Form reading. Clevedon... The weather has not been bright and sunny so much as luminously opaque and gauzey. It's been hot for what seems like the first time this summer and with that came heat-haze, so that the Welsh Coast has become invisible, lending an illusion of true marine. The bay became a dream sequence of pale blue, off-white, and floating green. As the tide was right in this morning the so-called beach became a beach, with families sitting on it, children throwing balls, and people swimming in the dubious water.

I waddled (the diet is working) down Copse Road like a favourite uncle, to see the forecourt of Scarlett's café thronged with ice-cream-lickers. I strolled – yes strolled, weaving round people fishing – to the end of the pier and sat to read the newspaper in an Aschenbachean kind of way. In the distance, the sea was almost blue, but close-to it was the colour of Duckham's motor oil and so, to the mind, of a similar consistency. I watched a woman doing the front crawl under the pier, expecting her to leave not

---

[30] Hugh MacDiarmid. Scottish poet. Another Marxist.

a wake but a lightly ploughed groove as a knife cut into blancmange. Pretty well everybody I saw seemed happy, or a least content – *at least not in anguish, Brian*.

I decided to have a couple, at least, of pre-lunch G&Ts (simultaneously deciding to take lunch at the *Moon and Sixpence*, the beach-fronting pub), and to sit outside the *Salthouse* at the other end of the bay to have them. *En route*, I briefly joined the crowd around the bandstand on which a Salvation Army youth band (electric instruments) was singing hymns. One of the singers was a beautiful black-haired girl in a short light-blue denim skirt. As I entered the realm of the imagination I was offered a song sheet, and I moved on. I think 'offered a song sheet' is a good euphemism for politely being asked to piss off.

Toying with the idea of also having a drink at the *Little Harp Inn* by the bowling green (good weather lightens my spirits and so they need tethering to the earth with even more booze), I saw on the grass beside the pub-wall a scene of such a Disney tone (the wild bull offers a flower to the sparrow), of such lunar sweetness, I thought the numinous day had seeped into my brain. Dave and Trish Bigwood were having a barbecue in their holiday gear. (It was one of those tin-tray disposable barbies.) He was preparing her some lamb in a pita while feeding himself two hot dogs. Kids were watching ("Geez a bite, Mister!" And he gave them bites galore). "Dunc, mate! Bon appe-tit!"

The Saltmarsh could have been in La Jolla, till you heard the Bristolian voices. The Bristolian for *Hey Jimmy!* is *All right, Bri?* Also said to women, I think I imagined after my second drink.

As I looked out across the bay to the sketch of pier, a phrase of Geoffrey Hill's[31] came to mind – one from the old days when he was readable by the average punter: 'milky with Jehovah's calm'. Not being a fan of Jehovah, I tried to find a word to replace it. It said a lot for my state of mind that the only one coming to mind was Jon Bon Jovi's. It was lodged there all through lunch at the *Moon and Sixpence* (I went in for the 'two meals for £6' deal, and ate them both).

Milky with Bon Jovi's calm

That evening I got into a tedious discussion with Shine about the relative merits of London restaurants. By 'London', it turned out he meant a patch of theatreland immediately about Shaftesbury Avenue, not even Soho, and by 'restaurant' he meant anywhere selling hot food. I went in with him to watch the news, and 'as luck would have it' on the Welsh BBC after the weather a programme came on in tribute to Gwyn Thomas. Where to start with Gwyn? Son of a Rhondda miner, scholarship to Oxford ("My contemporaries will surely have no memory of me, Eamon, wreathed as I was in a *pall* of tobacco smoke"), school-teaching, novels, plays, *The Brains Trust*, chat

---

[31] A poet, English (midlands), lived in the USA, now back in the UK as Oxford Professor of Poetry. GH has suffered from depression. He is highly prolific at present. He has a shaven head, in contrast to the comb-over he used to sport. He is a challenging read.

show staple. I was a child when he was at the height of his talking-head fame, but even then I could see he was a decent, sensible (he lampooned the Welsh-language ponce-ificators) bovinely-striving, over-wrought, and overly-self-aware windbag. Even if everything he said was not a half or quarter truth recycled, it sounded that way. As someone said (Amis senior?) about the prose of the Thomas we call Dylan, it was the kind of language in which it is impossible to tell the truth. I bet good money that he was a serious boozer; though surely not of the carousing kind.

Well, as a 'tribute' to the old smoker, they broadcast a programme from the mid 1960s in which he gave a 'lecture' on literature (a kind of what-to-read and what to *bloody-well think about it*). He gave it to a studio-full of, what seemed like, exclusively women, the kind of women who earned their living as tea-ladies, dinner-ladies, lollypop-ladies. Many of them wore overcoats buttoned to the neck and some wore head scarves. Gwyn stood behind an enormous lectern, looking suicidally grave.

"PO-TRAY!!!!"

He held an index finger in the air as if it had just been licked to determine wind direction.

"... is the chink in the cast-iron armoury of the stage set of the day-to-day, the meal-to-meal, the kiss-to-kiss world, a prismatically concentrated screen on which is projected the dark mysteries of existence, the ecstasies, the terrors, the possible nothingness – the VOID"

These weren't the exact words... but *you know*. There was much Shelley quoted and many words like *hierophant, futurity,* and, of course, *shadows*.
At this, they APPLAUDED, turning to smile, nod and comment to their neighbours. In fact, every two minutes or so he performed a similar windy eruption and at each one there was loud applause... "Now there's lovely for you," Myrfanwy said to Bronwyn.

"Now," said Shine, "that's what we don't see much of today – passion."

I had it. I would go to the 6th Form reading in the persona on an apocalyptic ham. I can do that. But first I have to get myself in the mood with something macho, demonic, egocentric. I think I should think Bukowski[32] for the time being.

---

[32] This will be Charles Bukowski, a prolific American poet

12. My acne, my anger

1.

for some people anger
is the arse ache
of the smiling man
with his pretty wife
queuing for ice-cream &
then going to eat
the ice-cream in the car. it
may make him snap at
his kids
or swear a bit now
& then
but really
it's extra-
neous.
not in my case
though.
my anger is the
FURNACE
of the milelongmilehigh
locomotive of my
self.

2.

for us poets anger is of
just as much goddamned utility
as a typer,

James Russell

as words standing ready in
the mind, for
it is the heart's prop-
eller &
much
the same was true of
beethoven, nietzsche
w.c. williams
& all those guys &
talking of utility i have
a friend who is a school-
teacher who
once taught
a class of kids
in which
two (yes, two)
of the girls were
called 'utility'.
so how
do you
figure that?

3.

nabokov said you read
with the spine.
fine.
i read with my ex-
tended
self.
that is to say
as well as my body

my chair, my room, my bed
my shitty kitchenette with
its cold cave of night beers
& my ja-
lopy
&
last night i read some
hegel, some kant, some
kierkegaard, some witt-
genstein & to cleanse
the palate I finished off with
some christopher peacocke
which you might say is
a bit of a <u>domestic</u>
de
nouement
(noumenon?)
but
who gives
a shit.

4.

i work at night
but
it is not dark as
my anger illuminates
the universe for me
to a range of
10
blocks.
oh don't

no really don't
keep your anger in a dark
cupboard in the dark
feeding it
cheese straws and dill
pickles
let it ram its message home
as my dad did
when he used to call me into
his study & apply the cheese
grater
for being late home &
this though i gave him
all my paper
round dough.

5.

funny how some people
can make you angry and yet
how these same people do what
they do be-
cause of their own anger. take
fabia
for ex-
ample
she told me that pierpaulo
sits down to pee so (
because of my anger) i
told him in turn that
she kept her pubic
hair cropped to a

number one cut
so that she looked like
she had recently had an
operation.
this made him laugh so much
he spat out his carbonara
all over his new cream chinos.
hey pp I said
dry it with a hair drier till
its hard
& make it hard as her anger
so you can then call them
your "relief trousers".
pp is ok
but he has never
seen dawn looming over the
typer at 4 am
as he sucks on the 4th
bottle of beer bearing
down on dark beauty.

6.

oh
i forgot: the bearing of my
acne on all this.
when i was a kid my acne
vul-
garis
was so bad people crossed
the street to avoid me, certainly i
had been long crossed off

all must-kiss lists. they crossed
themselves.
camus and Sartre did not have it
so why should i
?
also I had a stammer so bad i could not tell
my mum and dad when i had wet myself
&
i used to torture the local cats
with acids,
though actually
i made the last two up
& I did this because i am a poet
whose imagination is his 'horse'
in the phrase of freud (like
one of the plato chariot horses
maybe)
anyway then
my skin is now smooth despite
all my terrible and glory-flooded
drinking and my pussy-chasing
but
my soul is on fire –
pustular.

14th July, 2007

Easy to see why old Bukowsky became so popular: millions thought 'I can do that'. And they *could*. Also we tend to have a weakness for those who have a weakness for 'The Devil's Buttermilk'.

Well, I have to say, I pulled it off! I went dressed for the part – in a camouflage shirt, black jeans and boots, sunglasses. I walked up Alexander Road with Jason to Six Ways[33] and caught the bus to school. I did not speak to him (he was nervously excited), as I wanted to stay in character.

I began the preamble very quietly but would suddenly blare at certain key phrases such as THE BLOOD RHYTHM is the PULSE of the TRUE POEM, THE POEM IN THE DREAM, THE SELF'S HAEMORRHAGING THROUGH THE PEN, THE SCYTHING PEN. Some of the girls tittered, but I have ice-blue eyes that can flip from oysters into darts. (Yeah really.) Anyway, after an introduction of portentously bogus advice for budding poets I started to read in what I like to think of as my 'stage voice', which, to some, may be more of a 'room shout'.

I played safe with some real quality to start – Larkin's *Aubade*, and *Skunk Hour*[34]. The essential criterion was

---

[33] A roundabout at which it is possible to catch buses. Thus called as six roads converge at that point.

[34] A poem by the Boston Bramin Robert Lowell, documenting his time as a peeping Tom.

that the poems should be on nodding terms with Gywn T's 'void'. And I picked poems with that particular brand of masculine self hatred where the agent-self, the overseer (and transcendent god-like creative) is doing the hating and the self he is hating is no more than the common human frailty that even *he* has a little of, though much less than you lot of course. I then delivered two abdominal punches: Thomas, D's *Find Meat on Bones* and *My Hero bares his Nerves*. They really had *volume* baby.

They were a bit queasy after that so I gave them a little treat with a couple of Hugo Williams'[35] Sonny Jim poems. Relieved laughter. The sun seemed to come out. But note they had the *sine qua non* of darkness and masculine white knuckle.

At this point, I said I would read some of my own "stuff". The acne one was delivered at a sinister whisper in a voice I have heard used by poor Felix Denis[36] when delivering one of his void-doggerels. It is a voice custom-made for delivering the sentence "Now why don't we just let this be our little secret, my dear?" I dealt with the rest of the Duncan Pooles in the following way. I goose-stepped up and down the aisle, the boots coming into their own, as I recited them all straight off (only a hand-clap between) at Tom Raworth's[37] machine-gun speed. I poured myself a glass of water at one point and (another pinch from Ra-

---

[35] Williams has a column in the *TLS*. He won the Queens' Medal for Poetry.

[36] The owner of *GQ* magazine and many more things beside that.

[37] One of the few poets to have made medical history – as a heart patient. In fact, probably the only British one to have done so. No relation to Sophie Raworth (TV sports presenter) as far as can be determined.

worth) poured it over my sweating head, drawing a Whoooo! from some of the lads. Did I hear a 'Way to go!?'

And now I am back in my room with a ginormous glass of *Paddy* and four *Mars Bars*

20th July, 2007

Enough of this silliness. Acting is easy. An easy drug to take; and then there's the world of things you bump into. When I act up there is the glory and then I wake up a few days later like this... The sun has gone and the world is now the colour of boiled pork.

Shine has been telling me about Maimonedes at breakfast the past few days, about whom he seems to know almost sod all. But he surfs in on the fact that he knows more than almost anybody else around here. I pull a trick, thanks to a birthday present from Moira[38]. I ask him to help me out with some of the references in my copy of Yehuda Halevi's *Poem's from the Divan*. He's says he would love to but he must dash up the road to catch the 9.15 to Nailsea. Nailsea versus 12th Century Andalucia: no contest.

I have just read the previous para: Oh Craigie, what a tosspot you are, to be sure.

Let's do something Prynnish for Gawd's sake. Funny how this seems a realist move right now.

How did this all begin? In Edinburgh in the mid 1980s. The ground was prepared, as I had already heard of Prynne in the context of Barry MacSweeney (The Green Boy tells his Mother he's Going to be Oxford Professor of

---

[38] Dr. Moira Kahn, a colleague.

Poetry – Geddit!?[39]). Anyway, I saw a slim volume in a second-hand bookshop called *High Pink on Chrome*. The title was enough to draw me in, then I saw it was Prynne, and I dived, or rather climbed, in. While it lacked the famous high-pink-on-chrome dust jacket it had something instead

13: Clock Sure

The time as circuit spins sure to move
the baby size intent: present from core to core
as far inside the conker shell. These sparks
distant the cause to history fruition?
No one assents: the scheme falls flat from thinking.
Prettily on the rhyming scheme the clock accepts
backdrop markings; our wills do dream snow on snow
his dorsal drivel like paint that won't dry
or a song that kills the silence it describes.

Her son house fits neatly on the quadrant floor
while her eyes have the gumption, as t'were,
of "ice on tongue." His face thins out
the toddler crowd, its topmost rummaging,
cars on the office chair? He is firm like sugar
hiding in liquid by circumstance will rain again

---

[39] The 'Geddit' just takes the edge off this pompously ironic dig. There are references here to the late MacSweeney's first book, called *The Boy from the Green Cabaret tells of his Mother* book of poems (Rimbaud was 'the boy from the green cabaret'), and to the fact that BM's hopes had been raised by some late '60s would-be trendsetting Oxford undergraduates into thinking against all the evidence that he could be elected to the Professorship. His hopes were dashed and the poet sank into despair and further into alcoholism.

on too-green grass, each opened gate
or credit card for Scorpios. When you want
it there it shall be – the frame-warping faith.

14: The Talking Cure

The old man has prospects today
excited by his special lawn tank. See him
bustle from buildings, loving to shout across sites
shout news of their imperfect cubes. The cars in
the rain work round his sardonic mince today.

The old man hangs back from the lunch date to
cut a fresh slice off noisily. Computers
queue to his door past his throne, see him
yank a word from the cheek. Do not
measure speaking to his heart, right out skeletal,
articulate the cement whirlpool fast.

How can he endanger who is old? Who has
fluently begat all of his agents,
king to the carved refectory, crowned tight
for the Inaugural daily. Dead
skin adorns his flesh and his yet witty
nothings dig in beneath a flapping flag pole.

A sentimental look, the grace of age, not
over yet, enchants some young 'uns. The old
man notes their flesh and leans down
fit to charge them. His voice grates and
fouls an entry: his desk is wide
so wide he sleeps beneath its shore.

Fire drill comfort and the old man will
gather up his pretension. Some people rank
him good for gutting. The deck of rot
shows swimmer-glimpses. Crowds on the beach of
Severn pray aloud for some last graces
from his rowdy sentence-basting reverie.

that was maybe corny or phoney but certainly beautiful if you happen to be in that mood at the time, namely, pages stained a high though pale pink, like the papers of exquisite Turkish cigarettes. Why? I imagined it as being the early menstrual blood of some wraith in the English Faculty (anorexic, her final display) rejected by JHP for doctoral supervision (topic: Hilda Doolittle and the question of whether 'exists' is a predicate)... No, I didn't silly. The pages smelled of stale water, but then so do most things. I later came to think – wrongly, surely – that the title alluded to shooting up.

I'm in two minds about Prynne. On the one hand, this is serious, real-world-referring stuff. Unlike with Ashbery, you can't just relax and enjoy the strange *cul-de-sacs*, the principled evasion, and the turning a sudden left at a sentence's denouement, letting Ashbery-reality gently seep up into you. You can't just say "Well, I'll do with this just what I wish." With Prynne, while the surface may indeed be beautiful, every sentence has earned it's place as a ripple – *Can* a ripple earn its place, sweetie? – from a stocked mind thinking difficult thoughts about our place in the world. There is no surrealism nor gratuitous moves, but an eccentric kind of science, materialism, scholarship. At least in the early work. Yes, it's "packed to the gunnels with higher education" (Carey on Muldoon[40]); but why not?

On the other hand, who in his right mind is going to spend eternities trying to get at what's *really* going on in these poems? And where would it end? It *is* comforting to know that all these allusions and hard thinking are there, but – look Brian – life is short. Also, I'll bet good money that autobiography is the egg that binds the ingredients together in some of them; and I'll also bet that Prynne would disclaim his being an authority on his own texts. So let's not think we have to be Prynne scholars to enjoy Prynne. Ultimately, we would end up having to be a Prynne-who-has-forgotten-nothing to enjoy Prynne.

Given all this – as pompous explainers are wont to say – I will stick to the Graigie life-project as a man of the surface: I will use Prynne *prosody*, and nothing more, as the armature for my own words, slipping in and out of meaning as I see fit, lifting the first pass of content from events and lazily evoked concerns... So that... *drum roll please...* #13 was thoughts on astrology spurred by overhearing a drippy New Age couple in *The Salthouse* and #14 was evoking a pushier Shine as a possible colleague. (Funny to think I will never be anybody's colleague again, apart perhaps from in the prison laundry.) But stolen Prynne prosody all the way down.

After all, this is only to keep the Faceys happy, innit? ...not to mention keep me out of the nick.

---

[40] This will be John on Paul.

These days my sentences seem to end more and more on a dying fall. This is because I feel I am in one of these dreadful novels where nothing ever happens, and it's either a man alone in a room (*Dangling Man*[41]) or a bunch of bores in a boarding house endlessly talking up the significance of what they are saying (*Barbary Shore*[42]). I suppose it's a kind of hell. I am the reader and yet I simply don't want to HAVE any more reflections on this and that ... while at the same time I'm having to keep the novel going. So I'll pull myself back with another hopeful "anyway".

Anyway, I felt pleased with myself this morning, though in a slightly guilty way, after finishing #13 and #14, so I went to have lunch on a table outside *The Moon and Sixpence*. I only had one lunch today, but did plan on two puddings. I really am unrecognisable now. The fat has entered my soul. It's not wobbly flesh but good firm blubber, so that if you cut me there would be only a runnel of sap-like fluid.

A family asked if I would mind if they sat at the table, after which I could barely hear myself think. Mum, Dad, boy of about eleven and a girl of about fourteen, all dressed almost identically in those cut-off trousers (romper trousers) and sports tops. Middle class, no trace of Brissull, they talked in parallel rather than in turn with nobody deferring to anybody. The dad asked me if I knew what time past the hour the Bristol bus left from Six Ways

---

[41] An early novella by Saul Bellow.

[42] A novel by Norman Mailer. A flop after the success of *The Naked and the Dead*.

and I told him it was quarter past, to which the dad said "Yeah... right." like a spaced hippie. This made me angry so I heard myself saying to them "You can add the extra quarter to your trousers... Why not!?" I forced a laugh and then a beatific smile. The parents looked around for another table. Sorry folks, you're stuck with me. My blubber has made me more than ever immune from embarrassment, makes me feel invisible.

Now one clear consequence of my little joke was that now I could not go to the bar for fear that they would give up my seat to somebody normal looking for a few inches of sun in which to shovel in the stodge. So I called the waitress, telling her my leg was playing me up today and would she bring me a bottle of Pinot Noir and a Death by Chocolate and a Strawberry Cheesecake. Amazingly, it came so I could sit back and be happily horrified at the modern zoo.

The first thing to note is that nearly half the conversation was with absent people, by mobile. Also, rather than simply not attending to others when not interested in what they were saying, the idea was to plug the head into an MP3 player. These are, of course, cliché facts. To recite them is to name every blade of grass "a blade of grass... another blade of grass". And to list their habits, to abstract away from their attitudes, is to fail to move clear of the orbit of the thing itself so that the commentator becomes a player in the contemporary Hogarthean scene, the would-be superior intellectual drowning along with them. Oh let me give my choicest cliché fact, which was that the father had that kind of carefully disarranged hair, not Byron but William Brown, looking how William might look after the climax of an adventure like "William Drives a Bus" or "William the Pop Star." Dad ran his fingers through his hair, merely shrugging when the daughter said "Dad, I'm really fucked off these are oven chips". Then to his horror he realised he had just flattened his hair down from the 'William' and quickly sieved it up with his fingers.

I imagine the year before my birth. It seems a time before The Fall. Didn't Thackeray set Vanity Fair a year before his birth? (That has zero significance.) I think of myself as bookish, but I'm simply awash with book-facts. I am a big re-reader, a meeter of old friends. I'll write a cod-poem for Mother Facey about this. That'll show 'em.

15: Manifesto

1. Rex Harrison's recording of *Why can't the English?*
   lip-synched to a Hitler speech
   in every school assembly
   when we come to power.

2. My party will be called 'Nineteen Forty-Five':
   Mailer's concept of the 'Left Conservative' crossed
   with the essence of a rainy cobbled Monday evening
   hard by a tannery in a back-street with smoked
   haddock and buttered bread for tea, the radio
   and an early night.

3. Higher taxes! Fewer 'rights'! Lower
   expectations! Glasses of pure water held
   up to the sky. Back to whistling!
   And expert whistlers prized above singer-
   songwriters.

4. If you want a glass of wine, go abroad.
   No trips to France or Italy or Spain
   if you cannot speak to the populace.
   Linguistic proficiency level stamped
   on your passport.

5. Men to wear trilby hats
   and raise them to passers-by.

6. Bunting to be put out for the following
   revenant concepts and phatic moves: pot
   of tea for two; how d'you do?; a nice
   sit-down; chin up!; a well-turned ankle.

7. The digital revolution to be overturned.

8. The party salute will be a fist brought hard
   to the chest then flung out straight. When you
   rise in the party (say, to Level 6) this may be done
   with both arms alternately. Only the leader (that's me)
   may do so with both arms simultaneously.

9. You may lampoon the (all-powerful, all providing) state as much as you like but please never ever style yourself a 'surrealist comedian'. Oh, and the word 'contrarian' is to be banned on account of its plain sodding self-regarding idiocy.

10. There will be one TV channel and exactly eleven universities, with compulsory music and sport in them. They will each one have a motto taken not from the Latin, but from the work on J. H. Prynne (Liverpool's for instance: "The night is long/and limitless our greed")

Look, I mean well and I know whereof I speak.
You will vote for Nineteen Forty-Five and stride
boldly into the past.

3rd August, 2007

Why did I bother with #15? It's nothing more than a Jonathan Ross riff. But I felt tired and Radio 2-ish; so there we are.

It had started life as a little improvisation to amuse Sabbine. Not that this was ever a challenge, as she'd laugh at any of my sillinesses. She laughed mechanically at *Private Eye,* but naturally at silly dogs and her children's doings. And now as I sink into the post-lunch pit, sitting on the bed, hearing *The Archers* theme-tune fade away, sticky from *Mars* and *Paddy,* I think of her as a pure need, wanting the world to fit my mind and being quite unable to make my mind fit the world: conative and (I'd bet good money, given my diet) physical impotence is the destination.

Do you know what would be bliss right now? Whoever 'you' are. For it to be late Spring, a Friday evening, the sun is orange on West End[43] stone, the air sharp and buzzing with adrenalin in the Glasgow way, and I am getting into my car to drive to Bearsden[44] to see Sabbine and the kids. Even the kids' tantrums ceased when I let myself in. "Here's Jeckie!" in that weird half-German, half-Scottish accent of theirs. And Sabbine would tip-toe down the stairs or slide out of the kitchen with a soft "Hi there" and a kiss. She would look down on me (she was 5'10" after all) as if to say "Now what have you been doing, my naughty one?" Each time I saw her it took my breath

---

[43] This will be the West End of Glasgow – where Craigie had a flat.

[44] A suburban area of Glasgow.

away, just the very thought of my stellar luck punched the air out of me: the fine, rod-straight, ash-blonde hair, the green eyes that could flip between childlike and ravening in half a second, the slim unimprovable body whose low-slung buttocks – oh for God's sake! Coming back to earth, the trick was at that point in the evening to avoid standing in the kitchen talking, avoid kid's TV, avoid Sabbine on office politics and children's politics, and to bring her within the orbit of the back-room sofa whither she would bring us each a glass of wine. (Just nothing beats being *brought* a drink.) Ideally, she would then listen to me for about 10-15 minutes, asking interested questions, batting away the children and their interested questions about tea. Selflessness incarnate, me.

What is the cure for permanent, unassuageable desire? Come on, what? Spit it out! I mean apart from booze and death? Another woman of course – a *new rose*. Don't laugh, oh Generalised Other, but the mind has been turning to Mother Facey – yes, really. She is a strange bird, though hardly an *avis rara*.

You know how it is when it's plain that somebody fancies you and that gluey light comes in to her eyes and it makes you think, well maybe you do actually fancy her just a bit. "Fancy!" How old am I? (No doubt those merchants of neurotrash who keep floating past my vision will put it all down to those pesky 'mirror neurones'[45].)

---

[45] These are neurones that 'fire' both when the owner of the brain does a certain thing and when she sees another doing it. Craigie is wondering if the same happens with romantic moves: you see fancying so you feel it. See Professor Palm's groundbreaking work on neuro-criticism and her Introduction to this volume for a taster of it. [Cheers Claire mate! Ed.]

Actually, from the back – this is not an encouraging way to start a sentence – Jenny (her name) is not too bad at all. Her hair is full and sweeping in the country-and-western style, her back is woodpecker-straight, her legs are as neat as pins, and she moves in little skippy dance steps; for she is, if anything ever was, birdlike. Tiny, she dips and bobs. What a pity then that there is something of the crone about her face: the croissant profile. And what a pity her beak is not sharp and emphatic, but big and ambiguous. Her eyes have a birdlike sharpness, right enough, but it is business-sharp, practice-sharp. The little body: now *that* has promise.

I think it was the day I was dressed up to go to Jason's school. It was the dark glasses and the army surplus. I think I was also chewing gum, probably chewed with a John Giorno[46] stance in mind. Well, any woman with that flavour of C&W will resonate to a man among men like me, a man mean moody and malodorous.

---

[46] John is a poet, in the beat vein, but he was also the sleeping man in Andy Warhol's movie *Sleep*.

9th August, 2007

I would have done nothing about my Jenny-thought of course, but one evening, when Shine was outlining for me his imaginative "solution" to the "Palestinian problem", whereby the Palestinians would each be given a certain sum of money ("maybe up to $10,000"!) just to all bugger off somewhere else, like the middle of Australia, to pick a place at random ("all people of good will would be free to contribute"), Jenny Wren beckoned from the door of the guest lounge.. "Sorry Phil, can I just borrow Duncan from you for a sec?"

"I... um..." – I wondered what was coming – "I... belong to the branch of the WI in Long Ashton[47]. We used to live there a few years back. And, anyway, I still keep up my membership... I won't go all round the houses. You see I was just wondering if you would, if you would *graciously*, come and give the ladies a talk on poetry. Like the one that was such a hit as Jason's school."

I could have said no. After all, once is enough for the plausibility of the Poole person. But then I noticed she was wearing a pencil-line skirt in black leather and black tights.

---

[47] This is a village on the Bristol Road. It is practically in Bristol. Once owned by Lady Smythe, one of Edward VII's many lovers.

16: Human Sacrifice

Why rush to the unmet furnished out for sea then tickled pink then dormouse lost, your hopes as snow-shoes bang on skittering black as now. The whipped look and snug splint branches basically a pathos meld, cold air by her milk-bar stream: this quote's for you video installation too looped in an Oxford library, art looped that is, ground into she's falling over again again till the point is made. This is Aztec art, London Aztec, innards stained tannin ferrous blood.

Slickly petering out the planned conjunct cusp-hot symphony scored for smeary table talk too pooped to pop, not scored for horns tonight. Grab this flower, touch drool to kissy-kiss, as serpent gasp; would rather sit at home chewing bacon surrounding some yellow-sealed wine. Pursed lips post hoc in cab Thames bright, this mere memory sequence learned one glaring picture then another glory overlays the next, of priceless paint safe as skin under Aztec white mercury.

Well met at Waterloo valse hot friends in virtual cummerbunds (Aztec set inside the first) all set to scan peoplely opened wounds of the latest alchemist. Squat in the trench first, pineapple occluded, well-served to lure smiles from the ravening enraptured wind-stale lines. £42.50's worth of grief is not enough to settle down the systole to a rational trot, as if the Aztec dream washed up and over darker walls fetid was perhaps possible news within the fist: a flexible tomorrow's load-borne walls of hope.

Come morning, split-the-lip dim indenture to low-key instructions
from the fist, the morning cube will fit or fail to fit, project
or not at all the image down to south of river by clang and
clash of logic gates running from pause to potable pause projecting
the meaning of "visit" one that will fail to fit, sutured pain in leather
comfort sinks slowly before the idea of Aztec welcome, stony heart
tides back his needling curse to the the glial cell in which she lives
with the six year old's forecast of snow-fights and snow-flakes.

It's only pain's unbowed extraneous rant, plus three children
like three curd-flowers puritan about, sweetly over duck
lake to form. Make it over quick, this Cookham constraint sans
Cookham gloria. Walk germ-free from latency oblique to the
painted iron filigrees, commission force to flux and kiss four
times farewell taps on flesh barometer, palm away the feint
crunch down to the core, snugly die here in power ballad.
Some talk of Aztec she and really advert striate her phatic smile

but this water-faced interlude this mandible deep duff incursion
into foam unquenched this uncorrelation, germinal nodus, end it.
Read you and realed you on polished floors, lemon slice moue
to other audit in spiked fact sequence she profiles down the wall.
No blood basket nor hokum no chilli chocolate toasts just ice
metal sear on bum-fluff yearning rewind. Wrong body and
mind. Aztec science copperplate on copperplate hollow taste
books inlock a sensorium, slice chariot down next time a never.

17th August, 2007

#16 bashed off as a loosened Prynnish. This time I did not steal much prosody, just assimilated, as best I could, one of his later 'cross-word clue' ones and framed it round an over-egged bit of autobiography: back in my Beckenham days I had an abortive affair with a Mexican art student. Some of the currants in the cake were Wittgenstein quotes. Where do they get their marmoreal mystery from? Huh? Modern jazz themes were in there, theatre trips; but really I was just going with the flow. It reads more like cod Dylan Thomas than cod Jeremy Prynne; but it sort of does the job and it's not a complete free-for-all. I'll do a few more in this vein, probably.

But the immediate issue is what to do about this WI reading. Not the army surplus this time, I think. I'll go as a shell-shocked gardener. I really must buy one of these Mediterranean-blue cotton shirts like Monty Don wears, and a white panama hat too.

I'll be a kind of male Daisy Goodwin[48]. Poems as pills. Pills to make a loved-one's death bearable, to chivvy-up the mundane. Pills to give life the mental equivalent of a sepia glow or a monosodium glutamate tang. I see there is a new product on the market – stool-softening pills (advertised on TV with a table of ladies who lunch; nice touch). "Never have to say 'tough shit!' to life again. Try new *Daisease*."

---

[48] Daisy is a tireless advocate of poetry, as well as TV presenter and memoriabilist.

Yes, yes I know. Who am I to scoff, this master-worker of the cynical piss-take, of the mimetic nullity. *["Och, yoo're faire tae hard on yurrsel', Moira!"]* I'll play it essentially straight. Pick a few poems each about something determinate – death, love, loss of love, school-days, kids, travel (*it was cold coming* no doubt) and then say "Hey, look how poetry helps us to deal with/confront/come to terms with all this stuff!" A couple of months ago I would have done a shooting-fish-in-barrel parody paralleling the Bukowski one. Maybe of one of those poems to murdered or missing children that parents, or uncles (so often uncles), or policemen on the case write, to be declaimed at the memorial service.

> She brightened up our life
> Like a little ray of sun.
> Always bubbly like a bath
> She amused almost everyone.
>
> Oh how we miss her merry smile
> A-sparkling round the room.
> Her play-station stands idle while
> We all sit down in gloom.

Autumn is a-sidlin' in. Everything is sharper and more urgent. I feel *executive* even when my sweet goal is merely to get shit-faced and Bristol fashion and to thump cushions to Little Richard or Slayer. I sing along to Slayer's *"March on through the rivers of red"*; and that I feel no flutter of shame nor smack of irony re the latter tells me how well the booze does its job.

I would like to 'act up' a little at the reading but feel too within-myself when sober. But then in this state I do a very nice 'effete and wholesome'.

Big decision made today. I will make the transition from *Mars* to *Fruit and Nut*. More gravitas in the latter.

Wrote a sestina for 'em on the theme of coping with old age with good humour, which I make #17. I can explain what a sestina is and ask them to try writing one, get them to send them to me at Nimrod House... bored young mothers... suggest meet for tea to discuss. Have been listening to *Raw Power*[49] a lot recently. That set me off.

---

[49] Influential, iconic album by the Stooges, the band fronted by Iggy Pop. *Shake Appeal* is one of the stand-out tracks.

17: Shake Appeal

Fetch me my teeth. For I want to bite you
till you centrifuge to shards of ecstasy.
I used to be one of the Liverpool poets.
No I didn't. That was just a sort-of joke.
Yes my mind is a crispy crunchy heaven
beside you girl with your bad sense of humour

who laughs all night at certain modern poets
while tamping my old self down from ecstasy
in our home under the water's blue heaven.
So when I didn't come down from Liverpool (I joke)
I had a whistling girl who looked like you
(None can at once laugh and whistle: stymies humour.)

But I will not be buffeted by narrative thrusts. Heaven
exists on earth for those who seek the ecstasy
of the non-linear of high stasis. The joke
is on the river-chasers who think that poets
should sequentially – oh to hell with it. My humour
is boiling bitumen now. Yes I admit that Iggy – you

know "only five-foot one, gotta a pain in my heart" – a joke
to some maybe – was my cynosure in blazing youth. Ecstasy
of lotion aspect. The gym was my ante-room to heaven.
(Chisel flex torsion, I would have been the making of you.)
I worked out till my abs and pecs were minor poets,
a stomach as trapped bird-rows under silk. My riotous humour

Meant – look I don't mind; don't fidget! – telling you
that I even broke the rules of the sestina. For heaven
will not wait for those who mathematise their ecstasy –
dumdum dumdum DUMdum DUM: self-sense, humour
politese fly out the window when the chord poets
dance along the riff from Shake Appeal. This joke

I sometimes do may lack the lawn competence of poets
their preciosity; and screw their bubbling of good humour
('lean against a picture of you by my wheelchair'– some joke).
I will hang my leather trousers from a sky-hook. In heaven
they will turn white as white as my regard for you
Who pushes me out to sunny teatime for some ecstasy.

Humour-squashed smile, you'll get no amenity from me, no joke
no poet's aplomb. I do indexing not ecstasy
Iggy's not in heaven. I am. I shake. I appeal to you.

3rd September, 2007

I had gone off the idea of a little adventure with Jenny Facey days ago. The physical act of it would surely hit the spot, but the *ramifications*, not to mention the inevitable lifting of veils. And I shuddered at the very thought of pillow talk; and at waking beside that phiz – unmadeup. Yes, the neat, brisk body was wasted on her. (Are we all fascists when it comes to physical attraction?) So the upshot was that I had merely to get through the reading, get back here in time for a few pints at *Campbell's Landing*, then get up to my room for some energetic cushion-thumping to something meaty, beating, big, and bombastic, and more *Paddy*.

Things did not turn out quite as I had planned.

I came downstairs bang on 6.30 pm, to meet her in the hall as arranged, in my Monty shirt and my white panama, set off by spanking new beige chinos. No fear of being mistaken for a pimp. I really think gardening gloves and a bee-keeper's helmet would have nicely iced the cake. I saw her in profile against the glass front-door as a dead ringer for Billy Graham inhaling a menthol draft of righteousness. Actually, she looked quite formidable in her crisp suit and court shoes. We set off to Long Ashton in her little open-topped motor, not so much like Noddy and Big Ears as Birdie and Butterball.

Long Aston turned out to be more or less in Bristol. Mostly modern houses spun along the main road, inhabited by a smattering of toffs, quite a few young commuting couples, lots of retireds, and the regulation two dozen of the 'sturdy, unkillable children of the very poor'[50] who spend their evenings shouting, spitting, and kicking in the Co-op's limelight.

The WI meets in an old stone one-time schoolhouse. I modelled my demeanour and delivery on that of the balding, anonymous-looking TV doctor who seems to specialise in adolescents' emotional and sexual 'challenges' (boredom and frustration, respectively), honed for maximum re-assurance and empathy and uncledom. I could remember only the tenor of Andrew Motion's sentence about poetry being like a hot line to our inner selves, emotional cores or whatever, so I sprayed them with variations on this theme: "the leafy lane that doubles as an expressway to the deep source of transcendence which lies, like Jules Verne's sea at the centre of the earth, at the very centre of us" ... "a language that may seem like a code but that in reality is a Bletchley Park cog-clogged wonder: a code-*cracking* instrument that unlocks the numinous from the mundane." Stuff o' that nature.

Here was my little body-swerve about the Jenny Joseph poem[51]. It's clear why it's so popular. Timid women see the hope of age bringing boldness ('I'm a bit mad, me'); while bold ones like to imagine that it brings licence rather than ill-heath and loneliness. [*Och yoo're faire tae cynical, Moira!*] I began: "I expect many of you will know

---

[50] This was written by Ezra Pound.

[51] The poem is called *Warning* and its protagonist is a woman who decides to wear purple when she gets old. She will also sit down on the pavement when tired, gobble up samples in shops, learn to spit, pick flowers from strangers' gardens, run a stick along railings, and more generally "make up for the sobriety of my youth."

the prize-winning poem that begins *When I am an old woman I shall wear purple.*"

The older ones especially perked up. There was a general air of 'Thank the Lord: home turf'. Well, I said, rather than go down the 'path more travelled' (yes, they'd had him of course) I think I'll read a poem on a similar theme by Hugo Williams called *When I grow up*. Right from the first line (*When I grow up I want to have a bad leg*) the air filled with acid suspicion. There was serious trouble at the start of the second stanza (*If a little boy asks me the way/I'll try to touch him between the legs*). Two-thirds of the way through (*I love the smell of pee/Why can't I smell like that?*) there was rustling and it looked like some of them would walk out.

Why was I putting myself into this? Then, as planned, I asked them about the lessons for life – *When I grow up I want a thin piece of steel/inserted into my penis for no reason*: nice lesson, thanks – that we can glean from this poem. Nobody spoke; and nobody looked much if they wanted to do so for the next six days. I made the case for stoicism and humour – for humour-infused stoicism and a stoically zany whatshisface. Then I read my *Shake Appeal* as a further illustration. Well, generally speaking, 80-year-old ladies know little of Iggy Pop. Though some of the younger ones released knowing smirks; and one of these looked the image of Kate McCann (who has recently been inhabiting my thoughts); and so I passionately hoped she would take up the offer of sending me her own sestina when we were done.

I'll let you into a little secret, dear imaginary friend: the ladies of the Long Ashton branch of the Women's Institute do not, as a body, give a tinker's toss about the rules of the sestina.

I tried to rally, explaining that they had heard poems on death and poems on the world of children so now it might be a good idea to read one about the death of children. I love Allen Tate's[52] *Death of Little Boys*; and so I read that. It's a gem, moving and surprising. Things started well but they did not continue well. In the second stanza there is the phrase *extends a fear to you*, which I tend to recall as being *extends a tear to you*, so I read it as *tear*. I went back and corrected myself, and my mask shattered. I suddenly doubled up and felt myself biting the air, biting chunks out of it like a ravening dog, thinking in that instant of my father sideways on his bed at the moment of death, dog-like. I'm sure their first thought was 'heart attack' until I suddenly stood upright so they would be able to see tears streaming down my face. I coughed, blew my nose, left my tears be, not wanting to acknowledge them, and actually managed to read the rest, praying that I would soon see the *chill precision* of their *moving feet* to be *unrolling* away from me. I simply said 'thank you very much for your attention' and was met with rapturous applause.

---

[52] This American poet wrote some excellent (though heavily classical!) poems.

18: Extends a tear

Ample maw for now, glass new-blown
from the source shows a detriment
of spring colour, cracked and drained.
No happiness yet with dull coinage of drink,
the meek juice of the cookie box. Your eyes
sear your sockets' lash torment noted
by the primed-for-pathos posies:
                    as the armatures all implode
you empty out your middle brain, dog neck
the frame, then cling to the book. The kick-
started black energy emblankets the spitting hearth
as if nothing was weeping, as if these were
just cut-price but curiously bombastic embers
coming up for air. Nota, reaching
is an action moulded for pathos, its scope
swings straight from the store-bought hinges
like a cupboard door's transit. Despair
or dig deeper and weep harder, your axis
of torsion or toxin excites a contour
which looms sharp, instinct with dry cheeks.

I don't think I uttered another word in that room. Some of the ladies shook my hand as I left, often giving it a little squeeze. I half expected one of them to dig into her bag and give me a boiled sweet. 'Kate McCann' simply touched my arm, looked me hard in the eye, and said "I wish you all the very best, Mr Poole. May God be with you."

Back at Nimod House, Jenny Wren said, as we parked up, "I think you're in need of some *Lagavulin*[53] therapy." This took place in her apartment at the top of the house – a place as chintzy as one might have imagined, but dotted about with gym equipment, with dinky little dumbbells standing next to Dresden dolls and cold cream jars.

I tried to explain myself by inventing a son who had died of diphtheria when he was seven. (In fact I was still in such a state that I had said 'when *I* was seven'; but she got the general idea.) I wonder if children still do die of that. At least I didn't say The Black Death. "You're such a *sensitive* man, Dunc, *underneath it all*. What you really need is somebody to give you hugs, lots of them, and hard ones." She was melting. I could have coped with that, but what could not be coped with was that she was squatting on a rather deflated exercise ball and that these shiny grey tights she was wearing were not tights at all but stockings, stockings with white lacy tops.

Yes, officer, I can confirm that we ended up in bed taking the *Lagavulin* bottle with us – from which she took deep swigs in between going about her business with taut

---

[53] A brand of malt whiskey. Peaty in character.

aplomb. (Yes I know this is an odd phrase, and it's hard to think of a possible world in which it would apply, but since I heard it used in the late '60s by Richard Neville[54] applied to the Shakespearean verse reading style of John Geilgud it has stuck with me. Sorry, I've got to keep my spirits up somehow.) The fact that her long Dolly Parton-ish hair swung over her face had some aesthetic impact.

After, as we sucked on cigarettes, I spotted a couple of photographs on the bedside table of a uniformed male. He had Jason's *longness*. Was this her hubby, I asked. "Oh yes, that's Modrick." I asked what happened to him. "Nothing. He's in the merchant navy. Actually, Dunc, he's back next week, so you and I will have to cool it then. So better make hay while the sun shines – *eh wot, old bean?*"

The phrase 'you and I' could not be dislodged from the air. So – I will revert to this name – Mother Facey and I were now an item. I merely asked why he was called Modrick. "After his twin uncles Morris and Derrick. Couple of prize twats. Now come on chubby chops, let's make some more of that hay."

---

[54] The editor of the magazine *Oz*. A feature film is in the offing about the *Oz* trial.

11th September, 2007

Past few days: just as expected. At breakfast Mother Facey would give me an extra sausage or pat of butter (to go with my other five), saying "Gotta keep your strength up, Dunc." When we bumped into each other she would release a breathy "Hi there..." pausing for me to linger. Which I did not. I only have to keep her at bay till old Modrick turns up; but when he buggers off back to sea, what then?

Funny. When I was a Beckenham mod – and we're talking about 1964 mods here, not the later 'hard-mod' proto-skin-heads. So this means back-combed-to-bouffant hair, paisley-pattern shirts with high, long-drop collars, hipster 'bell-bottoms', Cuban-healed boots... like a pre-op tranny – some yobs shouted across the street to me "MODRICK". And now I get to meet the Ur-Modrick.

In honour of 9/11, I dashed off number 19 before breakfast. I wanted it to be a silly/bad-in-an-interesting-way 9/11 poem. Local, domestic, small-scale evil interests me a lot more than the other public, chest-beating kind.

19: 11th September pm

Mummy, mummy,
little Jamie said.
Can a decent hardworkin' bloke ever
lead an interestin' life?

Question-moths about her light.

No, sweetheart…
That afternoon her dropping buttons, and
tiny ruby drops upon her fingertips
smeared to workaday pink –
You must burrow deep
into a woman's heart then dig
a trench sweating with the effort
eight-feet deep and sit out
all other hungers.

Never fall over or lie
too long.

Never find yourself
on a stony beach at dawn
tasting her memory
dying
for a drink. If you wear
a beard trim it like
a local government officer's.
Strive for the continuous
thought to guard against
the moment, give your dress-
sense a narrative thrust. Doing

the decent thing is a matter
of attending the evening
classes, bringing home fish-
or sausage-suppers to your little
people their skins variously illuminated
by a well-made play or disaster footage.

But mummy what if…?

Okay Okay...
She tents the jacket round her knees
and pops a choc.
Tell her after a hot and cosy evening,
her head on her own pillow drifting soft
at anchor, that you're "going home now"
and watch her eyes widen like a toddler's
as daddy pretends to drop her
into a wave. That's
interesting.

Take the slip-road –
your silver motor a blade flash
in the morning sun –
back to bed from
commuting course
with the vodka bottle and
the paper girl. That too
can be interesting.

Mummy?

Formidable skyline minus
the Bugs Bunny teeth, the holy smoking
pain of extraction.
Against that
the paisley-patterned room gashed
with hell-slots and the spider god
crawling up into us is homely. Let's
be explicit. The sceptic
is right, the idealist
is right: the world is thinking
us a change of mind.

Anyroad, back to the issue of Mother Bird. I thought of pretending to be ill and taking to my bed. But the busy little bird has a key; and come she surely would to minister to me. The only illnesses that would keep her away are (a) coming down with a nasty bout of impotence; (b) a case of lock-jaw publishably egregious; (c) mashed hands. Desperate means were called for. She has to be up at the crack of dawn (*seep* of dawn?), so she turns in about 10.30 at the latest. Accordingly, I took to wandering the streets after pub chucking-out time. (I would surely not be able to get into a club.) Or I squatted on the beach or beside the Marine Lake like a vagrant until the early hours. It was so cold I reconsidered the club option; though coppers are often in evidence in 'em *innit*. In any event , she is not stupid, and knows when she is not wanted ("a rare gift" – E. Waugh). Indeed, according to her she has an IQ of 150+. Yes, I can see her being a wizard at Raven's Progressive Matrices[55], as a modular, bird-

---

[55] A find-the-missing-picture style IQ test.

brain skill, like navigating by the stars or remembering hundreds of food-caching sites.

She easily succeeded in cornering me. Heavy, irony: "Anybody would think you were avoiding me, Mister Duncan Poole." I explained that I was chary of our doing anything with The Mod's visit looming... "We're bound to give ourselves away, Jenny. There will be leakage. [A little smirk from her at this point.] He'll see how we look at each other." Her reply to this was simply "Bollocks. You're not the first guest, you know." Then I tried another tack: to be frank, I said, I was feeling guilty about bedding a married woman ("Not my style" – ha!), saying that it was a hangover from my strict Presbyterian upbringing; and that she would have to give me a few weeks to square it with "my God" (yes, really); then all would be well. Actually, my dad was a Presbyterian and an enthusiastic moraliser. I however happen to think all religion is toss and most morality an after-taste of it ["*Och yoour faire tae profound faer yur own guid, Moira*"]. She turned on her heels. This was in fact a splendid sight. As she walked away my Id (a.k.a. my Ego) said to me "Why *not*, Jack?"

So what of the poetic project? Does it still make sense to offer up poems on the Brother to convince Mother Facey that I am who I say I am? Yes, of course it bloody does. Call me irresponsible, but I don't want go to prison. But even if it does not, the thing has its own momentum now. And what else is there for me to do around here? *An' it's nice to have a hobby though, Jeffrey.*

"What else is there for me to do?" I write that and immediately think of what I have been doing and feeling at this time of the year every year, bar sabbaticals, for 36 years. Feeling an adrenalin breath coming at me like ozone, putting away my self-satisfying, slug-a-bed, late-night-TV-gawping self and gearing up to being Flash Harry, the eccentrically eloquent, piss-taking, Mercury-witted, soufflé-souled, outsider. In fact, I usually give up booze for all of September in the interests of sharpening up my act. Well, never again will I hear, as I pass the Sociology noticeboard, one undergrad say to another "Got tae sign up for Flash's seminars before they fill up."

It feels like I'm dead already.

13th September, 2007

Mother Facey (what do I call her now: Jenny? Jen-girl? The Jenster? The Face-Meister) is now ignoring me. Never have I seen a look so sour and so knowing. And tomorrow The Mod arrives, no doubt swinging down his bed-pack from his reeferred shoulders, aiming a baccy spit at the grate, happily missing, biting a doubloon and sending out for a foul with new tattles and a pint of sack.

O me miserum. Well, as a head-in-sand gesture I decided to cast my poetic net wider and look at new collections that are not modernist. And, franklay Bri, having dipped my toe in the water I've scuttled back to my *Paddy*-and-*Mars*(stick to what you know)-lined bathing machine.

I scanned the poetry section of the local bookshop, amazed to see, among the Pam Ayes, Hughes-and-Plath, three copies of a first collection by an unfamiliar chappie – good press, too. Reason: he was on the short-list for a big poetry prize: The Witherspoons?, The Preparation-H? Oi tell a loi: it was the Lem-Sip Poetry Prize. [*Fair tae satirical, Moira!*] I smelt a rat as soon as I looked at the back-flap author photograph. It was of a 2007-Byronic pose: dark locks over the brow, hint of moony arrogance in the face, open-necked white shirt, leaning down into the camera, sleepy-seductive but questioning eyes (all ticked[56]); but the question they were asking (at a crowded student bar) was "You look like you are in need of a drink, babe. Better yet, Roly and a few of us are gathering up vino and blow and going round to Podge's to try some *novelty*. Care to join us?"

Then there was the poems themselves. I had been looking forward to some old-style lyricism, something autobiographical, maybe some vividness, something free from preciosity, something that would not require cognitive contortions from me. But what I got instead was collusive fantasy and (our old Liverpuddle friends) A-level surrealism and light-satirical ho-ho. Now I think that if you're going to do surrealism then it should actually be either absurdist laugh-out-loud *funny* a la Vic and Bob's[57] Morrissey the Consumer Monkey or it should be done as if your life depended on it, or at least seemed to depend on it (Dalí). But here it was the soft English surrealism of those fly-by-night comedy shows that come on Radio 4 at 6.30.

---

[56] This single parenthetic word seems to have triggered poem number 20. Strangely, Craigie does not mention it and it has no bearing on anything in his life at the time. One strong possibility is that it is a pastiche of the kind of verse he was reading in the collection he is about to discuss. Or maybe it was actually not a parody but he is embarrassed by its resemblance to the kind of work he is now going to dismiss, so does not point the putative reader towards it.

[57] A reference to the comedy show from the early '90s – *Vic Reeves' Big Night Out*.

20: Ticked off

✓ Walked the Great Wall of China
✓ Currently single
✓ Well-known bingo caller

✓ Stomped on a rival's hat
✓ Presently in love with a hatchet-faced lesbian
✓ Famously turbulent

✓ Counted 900 sheep then got up for a nice cup of black coffee
✓ Now has a rose-pink battledore of a mind in a seminar of brown roast beef
✓ Notorious as a winter gardener

✓ Listened to a cuckoo on April Fools' Day all day
✓ Even as we speak is sprinkling cherry blossom on rogon josh
✓ Widely recognised as a permanent predicate

✓ Cried for help when rescuing a child from her symbolic play
✓ Right now recognises the folly of this act
✓ Patently a man of shifting qualities

✓ Rocked the boat which then rotted under him
✓ Contemporaneously she smiled on the banquette
✓ Publicly and with force they kissed as waiters fainted about them

✓ Gave himself the courage of a tartar
✓ As his cufflinks rusted with his acid sweat
✓ Now's the Time be-bopped in the background

✓ Greeted old people with an airport smile
✓ At the moment honing his skills as a de-peopled copse
✓ Cognisance of his cooking short-cuts was wide and deep

✓ Made as if all the city expected better, more life, more shade
✓ In real time there is more chafing than you could ever imagine
✓ It's as plain as the unravelled sheet: bogus copyright of cheese wheel

✓ Barked like a dog when held by his smiling mother, his spade deep in his bucket; and the weasel-featured man smirked his army-mate smirk

✓ Is now putting no further point on it oiling the wheels of the patch contour until the indent fury rests his

✓ Widely-applauded facility for living in the red silk non-existent folds of Saint Jerome's writing gown.

Wet whimsy without the power of its own convictions. [*Och, yoou're faire tae scheooolmairmish, Moira!*] Some of them would have passed for stand-up routines by Eddy Izzard or Ross Noble because all the verse had going for it was ordered-fluency, some restraint, patterning; but no linguistic adventure or curiosity at all. Also, it was terribly *knowing*. What's more – he said warming to his theme and tapping down his Meerschaum – people such as Spike Hawkins did this kind of thing much better in the '60s but without the dreadful higher-education-logged *cleverness sheen*. This is because Hawkins was a genuine outsider – a beat figure – so the content expressed a form of life, where here it expresses a career path. I predict theatre work, then movies (given his phizz and what he has said on the jacket).

Actually, I saw Hawkins read in 1967 at the launch of an Oxford poetry mag ["such as the University excretes from time to time" said one review; it never had a second number] called *I Ask You!* Spike was not getting it together so the editor (a Dylanish figure his friends called Acid Drops of Delicacy – or ADD), had a long confab with him. The Ed's face came up to Spike's chest; his hair came up to Spike's neck, which Spike bent as to the block. After this, Spike said into the mike "Drunk, says Keith" – and he was off. Yes indeed he did pause a *very* long time after the first line

> *Smiles, like cigarettes, can be enjoyed*
> *in bed*

and yes indeed he did (eventually) follow it with the last line of a different poem

> *leaving my lance stuck in his harmonica*

but come on!

Pete Brown raised the collective spirits thereafter.

These chaps were some of the nine-days wonders Geoffrey Hill not-so-subtly puts down in his new collection[58]; but they were *wonders*.

Also, the book was so timid. Byron'07 should read James Tate.

---

[58] Craigie must have been reading Hill's just-published collection (*A Treatise of Civil Power*, Penguin) in which he has a poem called 'After reading *Children of Albion* (1969)'. This was a collection, edited by Michael Horowitz, of the British avant garde of the late '60s (though including what Craigie calls some 'Liverpuddles'). In the poem, Hill compares the poets to William Kemp, a clown actor, who, in 1600 danced a Morris dance between London and Norwich. (It ends: "//*The dancers, faces oblivious and grave*/testing testing/the dancers face oblivion and the grave.//)" The dance took Kemp nine days. He later wrote about "Kemps nine days vvonder" to convince sceptics he had indeed achieved that feat. Contrary to popular belief, however, this is probably not the origin of the phrase. [The whole Th.R.U.S.H team chipped in here (except Megan), working the emails and Google. Cheers to you all!]

21: Are you a greaser or a stylist?

They gather all the pit bulls
from the yard, they like their desire and
music, desperately the catch in
the throat past dwelling on. The streets
lasso all tension round the hips,
concern for style, plus loved-up
with binaural sound of Pirate
Johnny Kydd here for help. Rockers blanche
at what they glean from contorted
fears; while he's basic fix-face
of the inchworm smile the now-is-clear
water-suit. Powerpoint shines beckoningly right round
his bleeding sphere, stutter out his
plangent harnessing. Think: you're the charmer
not mahogany but all entrained.

Camouflage is their desire & music: the
lake in Beckenham hosts all ducks people
will feed them. Our clothes Jack-in-the-green
as we shun reality bolus,
sensor, back-beat force, our master mark.
I don't know how often my mind's all of
tinker harmony all gleaned for my happenstance.
I see the youngsters come.
Our term starts an urgent, I offer
my soul-sense bisected, while the
lime-lights may pop out and smoke rise:
    so why does
    it hurt, seeping like
    pustule pack of coll-
    ective profusion, their

alters pliable meanwhile the table
turns and colour harmonial, as all
to compare the meat-in-the face: Full feeder, be-
side all the tiffin and tonsure. The
pit bulls are laughed at, while grime glitters,
my posture is maniacal / & belaboured
beside terminal hard-on as some
stars drawn up the ministered-to drunk chics.
    The days are stalling
    hopes with some fam-
    ine, why must I
    stand here shuffling, can-
dle drowned: is it now? Mornings bring a
fresh cause-case, but empty cups, encampment
by the mandatory nodus. Quick quick, days
slide past a public concern, why mention
the candle. All is wrack in this
inch of life, you snake-belt mod, see "creep
    to death." Those tar drops
    soaked in salt, no sea/
    sky line, see "Life is
good" by imitation, sealed up with smegma.
Asphalt on grass is the aspect & with
some cutting of sinews, renewal is stalling.
O bring me the order-haunted
of the despot-club, tell me my petty fortune
pray tuck me under house hold. I'm leave-
ing doing, da effert is impossible and
fuel of fate. I want return I
    really do: return
    and life, like you.

After that I wrote a Prynnish (21) and a non-Prynnish (22) both about autumn (yes, how bourgeois!). Again, the Prynnish loosely followed prosody and punctuation of one of yer actual Prynne-pomes (from *White Stones*). The idea was to bring together the life-canalising choices of youth plus the cranking up of a new academic year and all its choices and dread. But I had bitten off more than I could chew, as this stealing mode only really works at a sprint. Also it gets black and personal towards the end. Not a success. Number 22 was spurred by seeing some departing guests waiting for their taxi in the lounge.

I finished them, felt flat, looked again at Byron '07's collection, and felt worse still. (In fact one or two of them could pass for Mark Fords[59] on a very, very off day.) His will give *some* pleasure to *some* people. Could mine? I mean: *conceivably*! And what's worse is that this could this could never ever *matter*. I wrote what I wrote about his collection mainly out of jealously, at the core. [*Och, yooou're faire tai accurate aboot yurrsel, Moira!*]. Not jealous about the 'product' but (back to 21) because I felt I should have taken the path he took when I was his age, not scowling along Houghton Street[60] arguing with Durkheim inside my big black hairy head.

---

[59] He is a British poet and academic, referred to again later

[60] Beside the LSE.

22: True Autumn

Sliding into cold sheets the head cracks
the meringue of pillow, so only excruciating
cramp can cure the thought:

'I don't believe you: you're a liar'
He met you at basic Russian for sure
presented you with rose-wood-shiny shoes

buckled gold as a gambit, and now
won't even meet you for Kafeekuchen
despite your shared-essence-drinking.

Hot and dull hot and dull September
breathes smoke across the palm
obscuring lines of Will and Mind.

Take up the travelling cure sitting
tight to Bristol or Minehead delineating
kinds of truth and of ripping off, meanwhile

drumming fingers on Sofa World's best;
the taxi as late as death…
Can you sleep; or do emails squeeze

you so you feel like sandwich filling,
full fat and soft. The stone egg
on the silver dish on the TV

endures in green song, the right side
of neutral ground. Warm and dull
cool and dull. Let's get back to work
to find out what's really wrong.

14th September, 2007

It turns out that Modrick won't be here till Saturday afternoon. He's "visiting friends in Nuneaton."

Reading through what I wrote in the diary yesterday: sorry Norris, but I WILL stick to my guns about what I actually like. I don't enjoy Byron'07 and his ilk and I do enjoy (well find *fascinating* and quite frequently enjoy) Prynne and his fellow-travellers. Talking of the latter, I've been casting my net widely in the other direction – towards the Young Soul Prynnites. Jason has been helping me out here.

In passing, Jace is now my anchor in this storm-tossed toss-pit of a world. He's a nice guy: old-style polite ("Mr Poole"), though lugubrious and timid. He's thoughtful, and he writes careful, modest, clever little poems. One was a pastiche of a Metaphysical sonnet clearly aimed at a classmate he fancies called *Miss Patricia Barlow Selects a Word For Her Next Sentence.*

He's been encouraging me to use his computer to look for poems on the web, then print 'em out. (His room, by the way, is strangely depersonalised as if he himself were a guest. Apart from an impressive sound system and IT stuff of various kinds and a poster of Morrissey on the wall.) Before I started my little surf, he played me a cassette tape of Wallace Stevens reading. Terrible. Sounded like Gore Vidal describing scenery or an exotic party. What if I had heard him read the pomes before reading them myself. What would I have thought of him then? Huh? Eh? Makes 'ee think.

All I had to do was to type things into Google like 'John Williamson poems', 'Peter Manson poems', 'Drew Milne poems' and press a key. Came across a web-mag called *badpress.infinitology.net* complete with a spoof editorial, spoof performance graphs plus much toughness beyond the spoof domain: all the usual suspects and some who were new to me. It's edited by, among others, a young personage called Jow Lindsay who, from Jason's account[61], is something of a Dadaist.

The first book I bought after William books, books on cycle-racing, and directly after buying the first ever biography of the *Rolling Stones* was Hans Richter's book called *Dada: Art and Anti-Art*[62] containing, among much Arp, a fine expressionist poem by Richard Huelsenbeck with lines I have never forgotten:

The professors of zoology gather in the meadows
With the palms of their hands they turn back rainbows

(But hark! Is not the final phrase pure Liverpuddle? *Ach well*, Contessa.)

I've never shaken off Dada-love, nor would I want to.

---

[61] Why would Jason know this? Craigie is likely to be playing with the reader here. He clearly knew for himself more about the poetry scene than he was letting on. But see Professor Palm's Introduction for a trenchant dismissal of such autobiographising. [Cheers Claire mate. Ed.]

[62] Thames and Hudson, 1965

After reading one of his poems (an acted sound-scape of a dialogue between peeving adolescents), Lindsay took off his shoes and threw them into the audience. Also, knowing what poems the person reading after him was going to deliver, he read two of them as if they were his own.

Now look! This time last year I would have said to all this "How bloody tiresome" and predicted a career in accountancy for young Jow once the neurochemistry had settled down from its rolling boil. And now I'm a teenage fan. This time last year I might have spent two or three evenings a week listening to Webern and sipping Margaux, and yesterday morning I flung open my windows at 11.30, braving not only the cold air but the might of the law, to smoke four cigarettes on my bed (a legacy of my night with Jenny) to go along with four cans of *Holsten Pils* (and two physical acts which seemed urgent at the times and were a different kind of legacy of the same occasion), rounding it all off with an individual fruit pie and two *Lion* bars, plus cushion-bashing to *The Butt-Hole Surfers*. This gave rise to the Pantaloon[63] which I am honoured to call number 23 (some rest from the Prynnish). But really so *what!* And why was Plato coming to mind. Not wanting to believe that the phenomenal is all there is? The very *ideal!*

I have to say that, by and large, I prefer the white light of Prynne himself to the white heat of the Young Soul Pryn-

---

[63] Pantoum – an 'obsessive' poetic form composed of quatrains rhyming abab. The second and fourth line of each quatrain form the first and third lines respectively of the following one. The last stanza alters this slightly.

nites[64] [*Och, that's an offly clever wee comparison you did their, Moira, wi naerrie the wee-est hint o' cliché aboot it at all!*]; not to mention the occasional white noise, as Potts[65] called it. Maybe the season is getting me back into academic mode, but I find myself coming to think about how this kind of poetry is possible at all. I start from the thought that what might be common to all domains of modernist art is placing the medium at the forefront, or rather taking the medium as the aesthetic object. In painting, form and colour move from being the media of representation (of a man with a three-cornered hat on the back of his head and a long riffle in his hand standing against a tree) to being the aesthetic object itself; in music sound is no longer the medium in which melody and harmony are expressed... got the idea! In poetry, words and phrases (phonology, morphology, syntax) cease to be the media of meaning and the bricks and mortar of form and become the representational object.

Actually, this is all too pat because words are representational willy nilly.

---

[64] This is the second use of this formulation, presumably a reference to Dexys Midnight Runners' album *Young Soul Rebels*.

[65] This will be the late convert to Prynne, and short-serving co-editor of *Poetry Review*, the critic Robert Potts.

23: Lager Plato

Even as we are silent at home
Monsters are picking salt from their skin,
Ripping open cities for love alone,
Mocking our precarious potency, in fine.

Monsters are picking salt from their skin,
Flavouring for their fresh-plucked souls,
Mocking our precarious potency, in fine.
The juice drawn from our leisure hours –

Flavouring for their fresh-plucked souls.
Restlessness in houses, streets deserted,
The juice drawn from our leisure hours
Falls upwards like snow wind-thwarted.

Restlessness in houses, streets deserted:
A brunch of four cans of Holsten Pils
Falls upwards like snow, wind-thwarted,
Restoring one's faith in self and world.

A brunch of four cans of Holsten Pils
Plus four cigarettes, two carnal acts
Restores one's faith in self and world;
Beliefs remain in place like ugly facts.

Plus four cigarettes, two carnal acts
Make up the mathematic of The Fall;
Beliefs remain in place like ugly facts,
Battlements of knowledge surround us all.

Make up the mathematic of The Fall,
Make up some forms of life for goodness sake;
Battlements of knowledge surround us all,
The manifold compels but fails to slake.

Make up some forms of life for goodness sake,
Drink to the snow-melt from reality,
That manifold compels but fails to slake.
While all beneath sing in aspiring harmony.

It's mandatory and immediate to have a cow-thought after reading the word 'cow'. And while it's clear that a sound or a coloured shape can be lovely in themselves or dull in themselves, it's not at all clear that a word (let alone a phrase) can be so independent of its meaning. As The Thinking Man's Bill Burroughs (John Sparrow) pointed out in a commentary on the word 'melodious' coming top in a national poll of the people's choice of most beautiful word in English: it's not a million miles from 'malodorous'.

Better to take a different tack. And here I'm going back – surprise, surprise – to 1967, or was it '68, and my PPE[66] experience, and my walking down The High to listen to Noam Chomsky deliver the first of the John Locke lectures. It was an impressive one-way traffic of students, academics and intellectual tourists down from the Cornmarket to the Examination Schools. In front of me was a

---

[66] What Craigie read at Oxford: Philosophy, Politics, and Economics. The first is relevant here.

dapper little guy in a dark pin-stripe suit, with short, oiled hair, carrying one of those slim-shiny, leather-effect zip-up document cases. Small-scale business to the max. You could imagine him sitting down at the kitchen table, whipping out some A4 sheets and saying in a Sydney Mincing[67] accent "I am quite confident you will find these equity projections to your liking, Mr. Smail". Surely this little straight – yes 'straight', God help me – was not going to a lecture by Chomsky. He turned smartly into the Schools to be greeted by Freddie Ayer "Aaah, Professor Chomsky!"

Be that as it may, NC has always taken the view that language and thought are *separate* entities which 'interact' via an interface. The syntax of natural language does not seep into thought itself, about which we know nothing, really. Sentences *express* thoughts. Syntax and morphology do not make up the armature of thought itself. So, with one bound we are free! (Look, 'cognitive science' is a bowel-loosening word for me, and I'd rather not push the thought too hard here. It's too bloody late. I see a desert of magnolia corridors, magnolia chinos over cherry-shine loafers, serious beards, & power-point trees, on which grow linguists' embedded brackets, nodes and connections, pretty brain-scan pictures and words like RECURSION in neon.)

Free in the sense that, if he is right, language can be the autonomous object of cognition/perception, on a par with colour, form, and sound. And like them it can be fiddled with – moulded and maimed – to aesthetic ends, with

---

[67] See footnote 7.

meaning being an *interesting complication*; it can come in as much and as little as you like. We are talking about art after all. "The decision," as they used to say on an old game-show whose name escapes me, "is YOURS."

"Sure... but look, Professor Craigie," said Professor Royston Palfrey from City University New York, "but what about space? If one is a transcendental idealist, as I am, then spatial understanding is what makes all *thoughts* of an objective world possible, and yet it is often the aesthetic object in abstract art." "Neither here nor there, Roy. Now off you pop. I have more pressing matters to concern myself with. All these cigarette butts about the place. Must put them in a water-filled cup, add a spoon-full of cooking sherry and some nutmeg and stir under a medium gas. That's enough bleedin' thinkin' for one day."

24: Thou Swell

File surf brings the silt to light
some dust flies far from the pen
re-chiselling caracole think-move
present then ghost busted
by hand soothed with calamine.

This big & bold
move captured live with jet
fudge all about everything.

The horizon sinks to dead reckoning
before the swell of it.

Some prince cheers you on from the gone-by,
his cool purr, or is stymied
droops right slick to return
with precision stab.

The winter snow smothers
the point.

*

Some words fall from the book in nightfall
are blanched by remembrance not worthy now
but writing is your flight like a bread roll
across an ancient hall
is inflation from the sheets
when retreat seemed rock box.

*

Slouching that extra mile past hearth home
I am satisfied there are no children to which
Section 41 of the Matrimonial Causes
Act will still your chisel. Downsizing tenants of a
cortex coupling in darkness

can pump the production pathetically mild
mis en scène, 'cus after all the far-flung
ain't yourn   movie
bull-dozing the basic house till dust flies en-
couraged subsistence on brick bread (only
it's TV time Far East, move fluent to
big bold smiley).

The seen scene
although you may have given your credit card
details to the hospital, Mr. Jack Benny's professional
fees are billed separately and need to be settled
by cheque. Thank you.

*

James Russell

Botox sphincter, give your pen hand scope
when move a finger flood falls: don't
want the air soft consortium, diven wan' the
hard hour or hot spot, want D. D. Sharpe,
want to get on my pony and ride.

Some echoes are paid in full
chisel them

15th September, 2007

This is limbo. Weirdly, I have gone off booze. Though we're speaking relatively here. My intake is down to about that of Amy Winehouse. The sky is slate.

Bri turned to Ter, popped the rest of his corned beef sandwich into his mouth, farted, belched, banged his chest three times and said "You know that very clever and interesting personality Johann Wolfgang von Geothe was not too far off the mark when he said that thinking is easy, action is difficult, and to act in accordance with one's thoughts is the most difficult thing in the world." As we see in number 24.

I'm becoming a kind of poor man's Rousel[68], telling people about "how I wrote certain of my poems." But never was a *procédé* as homely as mine. This time I tried to take the form and prosody of an internet poem by one of the Young Soul Prynnites. It didn't take, and I abandoned it half way through. Prynne's language affords this kind of thing, but that of the penumbras does not. Had been listening to Bix Beiderbeck's[69] band doing *Thou Swell*. I had also been thinking about the kind of loose theorising I had just been indulging in and how it balloons up the ego and yet you keep getting washed back by the tide until

---

[68] Raymond Rousel was an eccentric French writer, somewhere between Proust and the surrealists, on whom John Ashbery nearly wrote a thesis. He dubbed his method of writing his *procédé*. Much to say about him, but really none of it actually *needs* saying. The poet and academic Mark Ford wrote an excellent book on him: *Raymond Rousel and the Republic of Dreams* (Faber, 2000).

[69] An early jazz musician, who was white, and died young.

you wonder if you have made any actual progress at all. Then something snaps even when you make a modest claim and the external world floods in – repression in the far east, my second and undesired divorce, my one-and-only and much regretted brush with private medicine: all raw carrots in the stew. And finally (how bloody predictable) a *cri de coeur,* a primal bellow about me. And it takes the form of an early '60s pop lyric, a little fave of mine by Miss Sharpe. I don't exactly weave in pop lyrics with the grace of Denise Riley[70], now do I, Kev? Circles back to the writing theme.

Shine told me after breakfast today that Modrick is "certainly a character." Oh *good.* It turns out Shine is a kind of 'friend of Nimrod house.' Comes here every summer (so why then is the bugger still here?) and gets on with The Mod famously.

---

[70] I turn to my colleague and good mate Steve Dollin. "A truly fabulous poet: adventurous linguistically but frequently personal in content. A professor at UEA. She writes big-brained books, too."

16th September, 2007

I feel sour. No, it's worse than that. Maybe there is a syndrome a bit like the one where the patient may think that his wife has been replaced by an impostor[71], but in which you think that other people's rationality and good nature and good humour are really just a set of well-learned routines wrapped about a core of utterly mendacious stupidity. Well, that's what I have come down with. This led me to recall a piece (in the *Radio Times*?) a couple of months ago on Marco Pierre White. He had been non-communicative with the hackette who interviewed him and had walked out; but he left a post-it note saying something close to "I should of have been more considerate. Sorry for been rude, Marco." Pity the note did not also manage to convey the pronunciation of 'h' as *h*aitch. Hence number 25. Harmless water-tread.

---

[71] Craigie will be meaning Capgras syndrome here.

James Russell

25 : Contender

Green light about Dave engages
his special cocktail of gin
and Night Nurse
I could of been a contender
if I didn't have a soul
like a walnut whip.
Dave before another seamless dawn
over flowers in their crises
the career prospects in the sea
of those night soils. Dave's life:
"lengthy, unmusical, and resigned".

*

But these are neither sham jewels
nor stars:
they are the real lights
of a distant city.
These steps and breaths bring closer
something that touches the spot
long before there was a spot
to be found: what is found
in the millisecond of waking.
There like an emerald
sometimes perhaps
lost on a lawn.

17th September, 2007

Same syndrome in operation today. Craigie's Syndrome shall we call it. I don't like irony at the best of times but *Big Issue* Seller's Irony' is the most mechanically awful kind of all. There is a guy who sells it in town and I always buy one from him and chuck it in the bin when I get round the corner. He must recognise me by now. But today when I didn't have any change I still got a blast of it – thereby the masterpiece of 26.

Walking back from my lunch-time pints at the Salthouse, I saw a family leaning against the sea wall by the marine lake. A couple and two infant-school-aged kids. The parents had brought them out to escape from being at home; thereby the masterpiece of 27.

I need to knuckle down with the making-it-newish project. No satisfaction here; but it will make Jenny think, against the fact, that all is ticking along with me.

Think back to the wonderful day when everything was 'milky with Bon Jovi's calm'. I was floating then. This had been a holiday from myself. Oh shut *up*, Craigie.

26: The Big Issue

If you don't mind no this does not
appeal this jim-jam of string ends
I'll work them up into an escape rope
cast down from the stifling bedroom &
roll in the wet wet grass far out
& farther.

Thanks mate. Cheers. Have a nice day now

Or better still don't even exist don't do desist
and slop to quiddity, chocolatey fingers circling
velvet cushions. Agency aspiring?
Might as well try to eat the bitter
flesh from your own head.

*Cheers very much then, mate. Have
a great day.*

Out of my face you gifts of mind
architecture, career fluction, meat-
and-potatoes sunrise & geo-swamp
out this this that & this.

You have a good day then. Cheers mate.

I never asked for the manifold was
never offered it on a May morning
before a blue curtain "in sight of the sea"
& what's on offer now? The food
scraped from your chin, canteen
medals cut from your eating suit.

You should have included an engine
to manufacture the proper tastes
in me.

Thanks a million, mate. Cheers.
You have a good night then, eh?

27: The Heart is

The chemistry of the house fierce as the wind
lifting the paper from walls of sopping fleece.

Little wood that wasn't snuff.
All brick tripe textured.

Words spiralled through the family throat
holed the ice air.

The bitch-wife called him Daddy Dinky &
the children played under the floorboards

singing loud gay songs to dissolve the pattern
above. Now, as above-ground adults, no home

fires can melt the core of them dark
wood rock hard wood, heart stamp.

29th September, 2007

Things had begun to look up a little after my last sad entry. Not-enjoying a pint of *Butcombes* in the Salthouse one afternoon I set eyes upon an interesting-seeming female sipping what was likely to be a G&T, looking bored, feline, and possibly dangerous to know. Late 40s. Long, just-off-the-pillow blonde hair with dark roots and – wait for it – a leopard-print coat nicely echoing the explosive stripes of her hair. It was a gorgeous day and sun was streaming through the windows overlooking the bay (not "milky" in this season but with shard focus). The sun beams were not like honey or molten buttercups or golden shafts of glory: they were exactly like ambrosia's shining gravy Bri'. So bright they were I could not see if she was meeting my eye. She went up for another drink (good sign: Gin and something) and walked slowly (padded) slowly back to her seat; but pausing to gaze out onto the bay.

Now look, I never ever try to 'pick up' women, apart, that is, from hilarious incidents in my mid-teens of clashing heads, spillage and stammering. (They jess fall into one's lap, doan chah know.) But I found myself standing up, then sidling next to her, taking a similar pose and saying "Beautiful, isn't it?"; and I said it in earnest. She slowly turned and said "What is? Your pint of bitter?" She giggled. Now put like that it was promising. But what I do not convey is the deeply disappointing South-Walian accent in which it was said. "No, I just mean life in general," I lamely replied. We sat back down together. She did most of the talking, in kind of kiddies'-story-telling lilt. There was something chintzy but pre-pubescent about the way she spoke; which was the exact opposite of how she looked. Oh, and another disappointment: she was clearly a hefty girl under the long boots and tenty skirt.

It turned out that she was a sculptor. Now when I meet somebody whose business is remotely 'artistic' I spew out all I know on the subject. In this case, though, it wasn't much. I find much modern sculpture (Anthony Gormley, the turbine hall fillers; don't know their names) to be products of ego-inflation – proto-fascistic. Beside this lot Speer and the Italian Futurists look like WI clay fumblers. But I was able to mention Brian Catling[72] of whom she was ignorant. I only know about him because he is the aesthetic *bête noire* of a colleague in English. I merely reproduced Drossy's[73] sceptical arguments re the sculptor-painter-poet; but did so in a tone of gentle, halting regret as if it were a position to which I had won through after much reflection, not a thoughtless recital of second-hand stuff.

But enough of this. We arranged to meet the following evening in the bar for a drink and "a nibble" (her phrase). Well, tonight *is* the night.

One wee problem I forgot to mention. She asked out of the blue what my name was, and in my excitement, and exactly like a berk, I told her Jack. "Jack what, Jack?" "Spicer" – the first name that came to mind; I could hardly hesitate now could I? Thank you, Jack, first en-

---

[72] Born in 1948, sculptor, performance artist, prolific poet, Professor of Fine Art at the Ruskin School of Drawing and Fine Art at Oxford.

[73] This is Dr. Drosden Gray (Christian name of Pictish origin).

countered in Allen's compendium[74] of new American poetry in some coffee bar, *Senior Service* in hand, before a black coffee in a Pyrex cup in the time before I really had to shave. I had immediately resolved to tell her that in fact Jack was only a nick-name (you see I had been mad on boxing as a kid – so after Jack Dempsey). But doesn't Duncan Spicer sound like a made-up name?

Look, what I need is a holiday in reality. Her name was Peggy. Peggy was a Cancer and "really liked Sagittarian guys." I told her my birthday was December the 10th – 1952.

Sooo... I was bounding (OK: bouncing) down the stairs two at a time. And – God help me – I was silently singing:

> *I feel lucky tonight*
> *Gonna get stoned*
> *And run around*[75]

At the foot of the stairs one of the teenage waitresses was changing a light bulb, wobbling on a cane-backed dining chair. A yard or so back from her was old Shine, living up to his name by glowing with good humour (or wicked anticipation). Between them stood a creature who at once

---

[74] The New American Poetry, edited by Donald M. Allen, New York: The Grove Press, 1960.

[75] From Iggy Pop's song *Fun Time*... It continues: *all aboard for fun time*.

threw my mind back (amazing really: that does happen) to my *Beano*[76]-reading days.

One of the well-worn *Beano* plots involved two little boys passing themselves off as a grown man. One scruffy Herbert would sit astride the shoulders of the other scruffy Herbert, the upper one wearing a trilby, and with a soot moustache. Over them would be a long rain-coat buttoned right up to a muffler and buttoned right down as far as it would go. This might have been done to get into an X-rated film, possibly called something like *The Curse of the Gorgon's Ghost*; but more often than not the disguise would involve the stealing, concealing, and gobbling of *pies*. The two-boy man would go into a buffet or a bakers. Top boy would look about sagely in his horn-rims while a smudgy mitt would emerge from about crotch level to draw in the goodies from the pie table. They would always – and this is the bit I really don't like – get caught in the end.

Was then Modrick – for it was he – a two-boy man? He swayed like one; and indeed there was a kind of hinge about arse-level when he moved around the chair. But no, dear reader, Modrick was not A Two-Boy Man. His face was that of a 'stinking adult' (Ashbery©). In fact, his hair and face seemed to be made from the same stuff; the hair was smooth, thick, neatly parted and grey-flesh colour; the skin of his face seemed to have been permanently deprived of daylight (did he spend all his time below decks filing?).

---

[76] A comic for boys and sometimes girls.

I halted before the foot of the stairs unnoticed for the time being. This is what was happening. The poor girl (a nice kid call Bonnie) was Modrick's butt and Shine was his idiot, lapping audience. He was making, and in the making his expression never altered, what the two men thought were dry remarks. Thoughts flashed by of Al Reid[77], a failed Al Reid in whatever circle of hell houses the masturbators.

Modrick's speech was broad Bristolian. His pourre wee wifie hailed from Bolton so she did not share that curse.

> Oi bet our Bonnie wishes she was playing gawf in Portugal.

> D'you reckon that if the bawb loits up when she puts it in 'er braces will pop out?

> Our Bon looks a bit different today, dun she, Phil? Yer! 'ow many loit bawbs do it take to change a Bonnie?

Shine nearly pissed himself at this.

> 'ave you seen 'er do 'er magic trick when she pulls a loit bawb out from behind Jenny's ear?

> I 'ear she prefers a bayonet to a screw.

---

[77] A droll comic from the north of England quite popular in the '50s and early '60s. His medium was the radio as he did not like his face to be seen. *"I've only had a pint, my love." "A pint of whiskey, I'll be sure."* That was one of his 'duets'.

She'll be drawlin' 'er pension boi the toim we gotta bit a loit round 'ere.

I expected that at some point this would bring Bonnie to tears; but she was clearly used to it, more bored even than angry. She changed the bulb, got down from the chair, and as she dashed into the kitchen I appeared before the shining twosome.

For Shine, this was the icing. "Duncan. Duncan, old boy! Modrick, I'm sure you've heard tell of Duncan Poole, esteemed poet of this parish." My conversation with The Mod went something like this (omitting accenting this time). During it, I should add, he hardly moved, did not alter his features from dead-pan, and nothing glimmered in the oyster eyes.

- Hello. May I call you Dunky?
- No.
- Oh, never mind. I'll call you Angela then, shall I?
- [*angrily*] Now why would you want to do a thing like that?
- Just joshing you, mate. Keep your hair on, eh?
- Excuse me. See you later, Phil.
- Bye then Mr. Poole, Sir. Don't let this here high wind spoil your nice hair-do.

When I got outside my first thought was of the famous poster for Skegness with the jolly fisherman dancing down the beach. *Skegness: It's so bracing!* Words to that effect. My poster might be: *Clevedon: The place to be a butt* or *Butt out in Clevedon* or *Butt in at Clevedon,* or *Mud, humiliation, impotent range: A pint of Clevedon is your only man!* The poster would show a portly little chap pulling on a beanie hat (radial lines from his flustered head) in a high wind, leaving a house which has lighted windows stuffed with laughing faces and arms pointing out a him.

But look, I'm Professor Jack Craigie, me. His fell wit, his sword-breaking, he the unembarrassable gadfly. *Flash Harry* for God's sake. Wasn't I? [*Och, yooure faire tae melodramatic, Moira!*]. I'd rather they saw JC in the raw after which I spend the rest of my life in a secure unit full of nonces and granny-rapers eating pissed-in food and dodging razor blades than live out my life as Poole. [*Aye, so yu'are!*]

But then would prisoner GH889900 ever get to meet up with – here comes a term once beloved by me and my fellow 12-year-olds – a "mature shag" in a pub with dough in his pocket. Not an amenity afforded in the scrubs.

Self-satisfied rationality pulled me up for a millisecond before I wondered whether I should have bought some condoms. Too late now. Let it be my opening gambit. "Hi there, Peggy. G&T, isn't it? Oh, and will I be needing some joeys or are you over that hill now, me love?"

I entered The Salthouse smiling,

*I don't need no heavy trip
I just do what I wanna do*[78]

settled down with a pint and simply refused to think about Modrick and the next few weeks. The refusal was refused. I need not have fretted about the condoms because Peggy did not turn up.

I came back here and wrote Prynnish number 28. Escapism essentially. Memories of a TV programme I saw a while back about Bob Dylan's appearance on a BBC TV play in 1962. The cold winter of 1962. I could remember well. Swan on the river? The idea of beauty and grace divorced from everyday mess of life (sometimes? always? spit it out!) whether locked in or flowing. And we will now read hymn number 145, *Bands around the Throat.*

---

[78] More of I. Pop's *Fun Time.*

28. "Swan on the river goes glidin' by"

That said, the sullen teal-coloured snow
    brought him the cold memory of dead
music from old actors; the men
    are bald to sing out and up

To find their cheeks hard to the
    lisping frame, their teeth gritted
as if nothing by proxy but mere parley
    tilts the Sing Out refrain.

Look sharp, this is the concern now, to construct
    music with a head cold and lust
leaning and sentient in thrall to pretty
    expressed for striped scarves, before

The skating cameras. Decide this or this
    meanwhile the milk's ice in AM, and
cold legs snap to some tune this
    black-board-like issue this slate

Chalking a sly Remington signage: his puberty
    with meek badinage is the route
to some delight. Meanwhile the swan
    fast in crackling ice-sheet, the earth's

Consumption and its clash and clay cycles
    right past it. His new bike
is an emperor's love-jewel, thin tyre tracks
    his bent body past the twisting neck

Of the bird-frame all gape and honk maimed
   with the weather's fortuity. It will not thaw
tackled with brain grit and cream blankets
   and teatime malt drinks. Why is

The signal for future dropping to track and trap,
   as if some happenstance writ small
to pish or pearl all brilliant and a bucket,
   measured round with damp wool, a simple horn

In the brown winter sky. Picked out
   in basement brown a spool memory thrown
heedless to red maw spitting in janitor
   entropy, it burns right to

Tar peg, fragrant and mournless, in broadcast ruminant
   oversight. Time is fashion, trope
to trope speaks out of sure youth
   gives hope to those truckle men.

Melting fast yet, songbirds are sounded
   playwright rhymes with vision encumbered are
dittos in a real too real. The hill
   is an anchor by fashion not victimised

As the assortment drips down and down. At the
   icemelt of meadow makes a conclusion of
simple stasis, floating beside all events
   actors in their stews in studio heat

Flare memory of boy-man, the song,
   the actor his split-off. To
conclude the dare-to-dream as the words
   freeze up apart from this and this and this

James Russell

Meanwhile the swan is free, tricked out
   in Burbery sashing though clear
modest and head set front, unreached quite
   from unstoppered, refulgent nostalgia.

4th October, 2007

The gay taunts have continued, at the rate of about two a day. Like most of Modrick's hilarious remarks they are derived from old TV comedy shows and the ads. One he endlessly returns to comes – I think – from Benny Hill. He refers to beef as 'beeth' and to chicken as 'chicking'. He might stand by the evening menu card: "Beeth tonight, as my posh friends say," he'll recite to one of the old dears who stay here semi-permanently. They, and of course Shine, are his core audience. Stands stock still, not making eye contact, and out they come from that slit in the grey ball atop his long dummy-frame.

The provenance of the gay cracks is predictable enough. Larry Grayson: I went in to the breakfast room yesterday and he called out as I was just over the threshold "Shut that door!" Dick Emery: I made a slightly salty remark to Shine about a news item and here's Mod "You are awful. But I *like* you." John Inman: one of the travellers asked me if I could make up a hand of bridge that evening and with all the shock and awe of night following day he falsettos "Duncan's *free!*" He draws the line though at the Julian Clary ("Dunc's just come in through the back passage. Now *there's* a surprise") style double meanings, but only through fear of offending his prudish constituency.

The only time I failed to spot the origin was when he saw me slumped puddingish in the lounge one morning and he called to Jenny "She can't even get out of her own way." No doubt this is a Bristolism. But note the clever way he substituted 'she' for 'he'.

I shall not lose my temper. I shall just ignore them. I shall chose my moment and use his weight against him, as Chesterton to Waugh in the alleyway [79]. Moderick is, after all, a sorry specimen. Never leaving the house, seeming to be incapable of the simplest bit of DIY, unable even to take a phone message, he is now Jenny's slow shadow, swaying after her as she dashes hither and thither. To his quips Jenny might say "Very good Mod" or "That's the third time this week for that one, Modrick dear."

But why the gay theme? Jenny told him she thought I was gay to put him off the scent – any scent there might be? No: childishly devious is not Jenny. Spite at my 'neglect' of her? Again, not in character. In fact, I think they are endogenous to the 'unfortunate ghoul' (one of Michael Hesaltine's this, from his comments on gawpers at an air crash). Mod must have a butt, as man must have a mate, as greasy noses crave chalk dust. And these days I must look like easy meat. And maybe he thinks that poet equals poof. (Or he is an Orwellian and has picked up the phrase 'pansy poets' from our Eric?)

The truth, Dr. Spooney, is unknown to science.

To my great relief, he came to see me yesterday afternoon. At first, he could not make me hear by knocking as I was filling the space between my head-phones with the Sex Pistols' *Bodies...*

---

[79] There is a surely-apocryphal story about Evelyn Waugh and G. K. Chesterton meeting in a very narrow alleyway. Neither could pass unless one of them stood aside. Waugh said "I never make way for fat frauds." Chesterton stood aside saying "Evelyn. I *invariably* do." [Cheers for the tip-off, Franny.)

She was a girl from BirmingHAM
She just had an aborSHUN.

He craned his long neck round the door saying could he possibly have a word. "Delighted!" I said. "Have a glass of Madeira." (I had been experimenting with this as a possible intersect of booze and choc-bars. Swiftly abandoned: *I'm a Paddy-Mars man, me.*) He declined.

"Mod," I said, "surely you should have said 'I'll not have some Madeira, *me-dear*[80]', with the stress on 'dear'. Look Mod, why all this gay nonsense directed at me?"

Wind thus extracted from his sails, I did not give him a chance to get to his point and delivered more or less the following speech.

"In fact on the subject of the taunts, Mr Facey, can I just say that not only do they embarrass Jenny and those of your guests who are neither senile nor absurd, but they make you look ridiculous. If I *were* homosexual, they would be inexcusable, and indeed marginally criminal; but it turns out that I am not. I don't think of homosexuality as shocking, after all there is quite a bit of overlap in the sexual acts that heteros and homos enjoy, especially in my case. It is certainly not repugnant to me; and I wouldn't mind seeing a bit of gay porn. But it is *unintelligible* in the way that somebody choosing to eat a plate of polystyrene over a plate of good risotto is unintelligible.

---

[80] *Have some Madeira me-dear* is an old music hall comic song about a old roué trying to seduce a young lady.

So please, please stop being so bloody boring. And what was it you wanted anyway?"

It turned out that he had heard about my visits to Jason's room to use the internet and Jason's visits to my room to talk poetry. No doubt he heard innocently from Jason. So the grey and snot-green giant hare had come to see me to say he was "not at all happy" that somebody with "the inclinations I thought you might have had, Dunc" had been "tate ee tate" with "me only kid."

I didn't have to pretend a belly laugh. I actually enjoyed one. I pressed a proper drink on him (*Paddy*) and we discussed the prospects of Bristol City getting promoted to the Premier League (goodish) before he went away.

Now all this implies he actually *believed* I was gay. Drop the mystery, Benji. It don't suit you.

6th October, 2007

Strange day. I was reading the *TLS* in a cranny of *The Moon and Sixpence* when my eyes happened to travel to the upper tier (probably cast there by reading some sentences about whether it was indeed Shakespeare who wrote *A Lover's Complaint*)[81], and there was Peggy having lunch with a man: business type, middlesome, burdened. She beckoned excitedly for me to come up. I went. After mumbled introductions ("This is Jack Spicer"), she sent the guy off for more drinks and said "I'll get rid of him in ten minutes, don't worry. Look I'm sooooo sorry about the other night, but I had a bout of food poisoning and you hadn't told me which hotel you were staying at." "Nimod House, Copse Road, don't forget." As she dispatched the man effortlessly I had the thought that she was a tart. Who cares? So much the better, maybe.

I felt a little inspired. She looked great: smart, well-made-up, glowing. So inspired that I invited her to dinner "as soon as possible" at a recently-opened 'French' restaurant in town. On the brink of a Michelin Star, so says *The Mercury*. She jumped at it. I did not want to muddy the moment by staying though, and linger as she discoursed upon this 'Virgo with Cancer rising' who had just departed (a friend of her ex-husband, so she said).

Walking back to *The Nimrod* in a roundabout way I saw something wonderful. A kid in his late teens was standing facing a brick wall rubbing his hands and breathing heavily. Suddenly, he rushed at the wall, jumped and kicked

---

[81] I am advised that this is not worth notating.

himself into a back-somersault, his shaved head whipping round about four inches from the pavement, to land perfectly. He had no look of achievement, though: only of watchful stillness. I applauded. "Cheers pal," he said. This was my happiest moment since coming to Clevedon. But I immediately thought of the kind of action that was the symmetrical opposite to this: middle-class internet dating. Hence number 29. Bit of a Prynnish, as I did nick a bit of prosody from *High Pink on Chrome*. I mean, fair cop guv.

29: Ullage

He makes the spin ex nihilo, swings low
    the air round bare head; this gulp of
scally-swipe up to gravity. Thus
    is tokened a what-to-do, a swatch
of that which homes on cement, stone free.

Weekends roll by, the café is talking
    wine dregs are washed with thought.
They smirk to please in clothes
that wrap a soufflé, walking to the
    earth tug. She lolls in her looks

and dreams of a man, drops into
    gear for some kind soul, is fearful but
shouting her worth of sex to the tappers
    scratching for favour: there are some left
some even normally hacked in life.

Frankly there are no turns, no tumblings
    over drop or on stone passage.
What is left is schwer and bruise-dark, dog
    sniff to canteen excretions. Cheers then!
Some one will turn up to your log, desire,
    Suffice – soul of your soul, right?

8th October, 2007

My principal memory of this day: staring at an enormous oval plate, hoping the hot air from the mouth of my dining companion would dry the gathering tears of boredom, and contemplating a piece of pheasant about the size of a field-mouse surrounded by red and green curlicues. By the end of the day, I was that field-mouse, your honour.

The day had started well, the glow from The Glorious Sixth still within me. I hardly ate (by my standards) all day to sharpen my appetite. Maybe – I thought away while my higher self said 'bollocks!' – Peggy was the well of company and comfort that I needed. But what if she phoned Nimrod House one day and asked to speak to "Jack Spicer"? No matter: I was carefree.

We met in a wine-bar near the restaurant. Large gins and tonics were consumed, twice over. Oh she was smart enough to look at, but with the too-familiar, bedraggled mind, like an unmade bed, one which covered the whole ground-floor of the house, with people coming and going over it from front to back and back again.

The question at this point: Why report the change in rhythm of a dripping tap?

Peggy talked not about sculpture, nor about how things were with her, not even about her day; and showed not the slightest curiosity about me. She talked about her work-mates from the days when she was in the Bristol *Debenhams*. I heard in fluently devastating detail about the schooling of the children of people I would never meet (Elaine, Charlie, Suzi, Dave, and Gary), about one of their cousins who may or may not have got a place to read Psychology at the University of Hertfordshire. She was not a listener then, so I decided I would not be one either, and attended over her shoulder.

There was a couple in the bar who were obviously on a blind date, no doubt internetly arranged. He was talking out at the air too rapidly while she watched him appraisingly with a bland but curdling smile. He was over-weight and his every gesture and glance spoke of a floundering that stretched beyond this meeting. High stools to a minimalist table plus large glasses, of what I recently heard dubbed 'lady petrol'[82] was their ingle nook; but not even Betjeman[83] could have found wry humour or universality in this scene. It may well *become* universal though. I went back to listening to mah Peggy'o.

A new word was now peppering her monologue – 'pash' (for passion). Not actual passion: just fancying somebody. You see Gary has a pash for Elaine, while Elaine had one of those pashes for Dave. "And where" – I thought I'd try a wry, dry, crisp, and spry witticism, just to witness its effect – "would The Western Canon be if that were not ever the case!" She paused, did not say "What canon?", swigged her G&T and said "You're not wrong there, Jack."

As she continued I imagined (for reasons far beyond the reach of science) what it would have been like, one work-

---

[82] That is, white wine.

[83] Craigie is referring here to one of John Betjeman's best-loved poems *In a Bath Tea Shop*.

ing afternoon in the Adam Smith Building[84], to spend some time doing the breaststroke (how would the front crawl have worked, I wonder?) along the corridors and down the stairs. The corridors outside the lecturers' offices were so narrow that I could have propelled myself quite nicely using my feet against the walls. Imagine swimming into a lift and lying there holding a conversation, then swimming out: Ah, that's my floor! The reactions of my colleagues and students: "Nice day for it, Jack"; "Are you being a subject in a psychology experiment again, Jack?"; "You'll ruin that lovely suit, ya wee vampot!"; "Are you the new floor polisher, Professor Craigie?". Then as I was hearing the buttons of my jacket pop off as I flopped down the stairs like something between a Guy Fawks and a seal I came to, for Peggy had paused. "Well, Jack, *do* you think Pete Doherty is on the 'highway to hell', as Suzi calls it?"

Then a bit later she asked me my opinion again. "So, come on, Jack, would you say Elaine was *living the dream* then or not?" I confessed archly that I had no idea what the phrase meant. People said it to one another when they didn't quite know what else to say: "We've just bought a caravanette![85]" "Live the dream, Elvin." At which she told me she could "just imagine" me as a school master. (I'd had said I was a retired English teacher from Tufnell Park.) This was because – said she – I was given to formulations like 'If A says to B' or 'If you did X and I did Y'. "Let's go and eat", said I. "You mean A and B are going to do X" (she was better when tiddly). "And they

---

[84] See footnote 20.

[85] What, in the USA, would be called a winnebago.

might later do Y", was my retort. She slapped me on the arm: "Cheeky monkey!"

We were greeted at the door by a muscle-bound youth in what looked like fancy dress. Strangled by his collar, his face as red and spotty as his bow-tie.

M-B.Y: Good evenin', Sir, Madam.
J.C: All right, Bri?

I didn't know what I was saying as I was thinking about the prospects of later Y.
M-B.Y didn't flinch, assuming that this was how I actually spoke.

I love eating in restaurants new to me because... Oh, never mind.

I ordered a Rioja, and we started a second bottle when the main course dropped in front of us. I was starving, but the portions... day wear bleedin' diabolical. I kept ordering bread and promising myself two, or maybe three, puddings. I was seriously considering nipping across the road for a pastie or twain.

Peggy was talking less now, but it was all about past lovers – the Sagittarians and all the rest of 'em. Up to a certain point in the meal I had been feeling mellow, though with an unfocussed, risk-red, domain-general hunger. That point being, Seamus? When she began to describe in grinding detail her time with a lover called 'Dave B'. No, not the Dave from Gentlemen's Fashions, but a Dave I thought I knew. "Do you mean Dave *Bigwood*, by any chance?" "How do you know Big Dave?" I explained (even the barbecue). It turned out that Dave had picked her up in a Bristol wine bar. "Just like you, Jack. I don't know what it is... [a fey toss of the leopard hair]... but men are always hitting on me". *Hitting on me!* And 'hitting' was pronounced 'hetting'. "How do you mean *'hetting'* on you?" She wasn't listening.

The affair with Dave the 'Sag' had continued for about six months "till I moved on." Where? To the Salthouse to join the afternoon men[86]. "He was an ANimal in bed, Jack!" "What sort? Capybara? Slow worm?" "No, silly – a LEI-on." He had been coming round to service her during the recent visit, telling Trish he had to nip back to the office to "TRUB-ALL-shoot". He even managed a quickie when Trish was selecting presents in the pottery round the corner from Nimrod. "It was so exSITEin'. I can TELL you."

So that was Dave Bigwood then. Silly old me for having put him down as sweetly naïve, boyish, magnanimous, tough-guy source of sunshine, a fine mentor to his graduate students whom I can recommend to you as a serious candidate for this Lectureship. How shall I think of him now? [*Och! As a nasty wee thing, Moira.*] But he wasn't really the issue here at all at all at all. Trish was the issue. Shall I say why and douse her too with predicates? No! Just use your *imagination*. My thought was as finely nuanced, in fact, as 'woman is the nigger of the world'[87].

---

[86] Probably a reference to a novel by Anthony Powell about the denizens of a Soho drinking club.

[87] A song by John Lennon.

Peggy could tell something has gone wrong with me. In fact, *mirabile dictu* (as they say in *Campbell's Landing*), she began to ask me about myself, so that eventually I found myself going on about my second marriage and how it ended with a jolt one Easter with her telling me to sling my hook; though in the language of an international lawyer with a Ph.D. in linguistic philosophy. The fact is that this diamond blonde could almost certainly have beaten me up. I tried to joke... "But I had the speed, so I was tempted to insult her and then run away." "Were you, Jack? *Were* you?" She was holding one of my hands and stroking it, gazing into my eyes like a police psychologist. She had hands the texture of emery board. "Eat up your pud, Jack. I'll take you back to see my sculptures."

In the taxi I said "This reminds me of the New Yorker cartoon about a man invited back by a girl to see her etchings. He wasn't very keen, so he said in the lobby of her building 'Couldn't you just bring the etchings down?'" She had not drunk enough not to be insulted by this. "I don't *get* you sometimes, Jack." Clearly, I *had* drunk enough to be casually insulting. And anyway, I *was* in two minds about this project; though in one of the minds my breathing was fast and shallow and had me squeezing her thigh.

The sculptures were a blur of half-finished half-thoughts. Look, I have been giving this girl too hard a time already and there is harder time to come, so I won't dwell on these art works. More to the point, we were bad lovers that night. When she came back from the bathroom naked, I experienced *a death of the spirit*, a phrase lodged within me since 1971 when I heard it used, in a production of the James Joyce play *Exiles* – by T.P. McKenna, playing a friend of the protagonist. He used to describe what had happened to him one night in Paris riding home in a cab with a tart. (All this I thought in 250 milliseconds.)

She was big, rubbery and, as it turned out, un-aroused. And dramatically pot bellied. So that was why she wore those enormous belts over her dresses, belts on the Lonsdale[88] scale. In fact, when she was taking off her leopard-skin coat I had imagined a Kray twin on either side of her each holding an arm aloft and declaring her Champeen. Her role in the act itself paralleled that of a piece of gym equipment, with settings for 'resistance', 'speed', and 'incline'. At the end (my end) she asked if I'd like to stay the night. I declined, lying that I suffered from 'spondylosis of the neck' and could only sleep on the specially-sculpted pillow which resided at the *Nimrod*. "When he comes/he goes" as another Hugo Williams poem has it. Or...

I bid good night
To the blonde bombsite

I walked home feeling like a character in a Kingsley Amis novel or indeed a KA poem. And thus number 30.

---

[88] This is a boxing belt, inaugurated by Lord Lonsdale (president of the National Sporting Club of Britain) in 1909. If a boxer became champion and defended his title successfully three times he won the belt.

30: An Old Devil's Stag Night

There in the bar wettening
themselves with good hope pushing
age away before dinner. Just

pay the silly bill old chum &
thread with her back to your
discovery, amid those oh-too-solid

flesh hills, of the small
smile of clough, its cache
of bones ground down to face

powder. For this is your marrow
matey: impacted wine-red dregs
& gin-sour mash. You'll travel-read

the night away, you'll turn the page
to see the Column of Columbus
veiled, pointing just as far

as Majorca & its sun shades, towards
another weeping woman, one amicable as
pudding, but with your measure.
Oh it wasn't
a bad night old cock, buck up
old son.

15th October, 2007

While I have lived a creature of the common room surrounded by intelligent people (some of them also being young, sparky women) and general conversation of an impersonal kind, I now have a social life serially: two middle-aged women, an old man, an adolescent male, an idiot male. But what am I? Jack Craigie is dead and Duncan Poole is a nasty clown who lives in the wardrobe. The fact is that the creature that now sleeps in my room is a soft man, a man of eating, drinking, lying, and hiding. But then wasn't Jack Craigie a soft man too? A physical coward at the still point of converging appetites. Vain to absurdity, overdressed, and prattling. Forever reprising Oxford in the late '60s, London in the early '70s, telling self-aggrandising stories about Freddie Ayer, Robin Blackburn[89], willing postgraduettes, about meeting Keith Richards in a Chichester pub and discussing *The Hand of Fate*[90] while sharing a plate of chips. I have fallen, and this is its mathematic, within the ambit of Jos Sedley[91]. In short, I have come home to roost, my taste, as with Sedley, for hot curry intact.

"What's wrong with the Jos Sedleys?" You may ask. They are soft when the world is hard, sweet when the world tastes of salty blood. Which thought, in a vague way gave rise to 31, or more accurately *arose from its writing*. I

---

[89] A prominent British socialist, who taught Sociology at the LSE in the 1960s, where he famously supported a sit-in.

[90] A soul-stirring Rolling Stones track from the album *Black and Blue*.

[91] Jos Sedley is a character in Thackeray's Vanity Fair -- a weakling glutton.

will come clean (why? nobody else does)... some prosody
burgle from two pages of *The Oval Window* [92].

31: Sweet Water

On the margin of a couchant fate
we are welcomed sunnily by the
    kind benighted, puckered proud
around it - the sweet water flow.

We glowing and quite fitful, ours
a fine remembering how to love
    the sweet nurture
smiling its mark, frayed as they come.

The bank extends to the trenchant
sea all moss smeared flat, our features reflect
    "quite nicely" our day fuel
and, yes, our bleached accord. All look

for the pearly path, find it falling
dead near some grinding calm. Tension
    cold-call, trick-treat for
greater care, we all sup simple sauce

---

[92] A long poem by J. H. Prynne.

James Russell

and its harbour-light. He stuffs bags
till they conceal groin; he stands a Brummel beacon
    goose-fat on his tonsils,
his wrinkled nose caused the stink.

His outfit shines out with the top down
gorged those legs-as-bodies. "Hark my friend
    to my tales." His lovers
are waistcoats, boot muster he slicks up

always sups to the dredgings. Stands his ground
fire-side, environs immured from slight
    charms a baby, in-
deed, he loves all nice in the room.

***

One day a war was caused and pain and blood
while London marched on fudge, there runnelled
    guts and cries abroad,
him-goading till the flight to find

the fun to watch from a war horse.
His face hair adorned break-a-fast here, see
    his countenance in melt up to
smoke. He a real-stone kicker!

Or a fire starter! He the sweet heir
of a lush-in-the-loins florist,
    dressed loud laughing.
Scones are late in the murderous lounge

party-wrecked, telling him the all-known:
that the world can cause you, babba, to cease
    to be on this little trip –
no patties, no Malmsey. This is proof

as, limp from thinking, the thought is
plane as muffin ash. All who trouble
    the courts with world-doubting
will face a wind of nihil; for

the causal power is stone right into
the tender, and monkey-browed
    they'll lose quality.
He fears for his sensory fields and tries

to buy a horse, rides all toad in hardening hours, hard as
ending too soon. Straight home
    to his soft hearth
with its sweet science, to try a pure lie.

Salt in throat, drowned by the living.
Thus was he born: the care too strong,
    with careless action holy, when
the carefree sword swings by the sucking pig.

18th October, 2007

I feel so happy I think I'll sing a song. No I won't. Instead I'll do the twist to *Do the Hucklebuck*[93] playing in my imagination.

That really is enough irony for one day. Today something impossible happened, something impossibly bad. I saw a picture of Sabbine and The Toilet on the front of the *Sun*.

I'll explain who The Toilet is later. The bare facts are these. I walked up Alexander Road to get my morning *Guardian* after breakfast, and there on the board outside a splayed *Sun* and the words

Sab did it!

If you looked closely you could see faint grey quotation marks in the black background. And there was Sabbine getting out of The Toilet's *Mercedes*.

Sorry, but an account of The Toilet, of who he is, and of his role in Sabbine's life will have to wait until I ink in Sabbine herself, my partnership with her and the murder. I'm not ready for that yet.

I will, though, say this 'just now' (in the words of The Godhead Desmond Carrington[94]) about The Toilet: that

---

[93] Craigie is likely to be thinking here of the hit recording of this song by an Irish showband – The Royal Show Band of Waterford.

[94] Carrington is a Radio 2 disc jockey of the older generation. He ends his programmes with "Bye just now" See poem number 2.

there is nothing particularly lavatorial about him and that the nickname I coined was reached by two stepping stones (one a phonological parallel and one rhyming slang). His real name is Dr. Barry Ritter so I – of course! – came to refer to him as Garry Glitter, shortened to 'Gary'; after which, to my complete delight, I discovered that 'the Gary' is the rhyming slang for a toilet, with Gary Glitter = shitter.

Anyway (what a useful word that is), *The Sun* must have been suffering a low news day... As the Madeleine McCann[95] abduction had had the scrapings of its scraping scraped, they were stuck with the seemingly open-and-shut case of the 4-year-old boy who was murdered in Glasgow. The mother's boy-friend (John 'Jack' Craigie, Professor of Social Theory) who had been in the house at the time went missing – so I understand. Why did they prize it open? Because of Sabbine herself of course: somebody born to emerge through dry ice wearing a black leather bikini and a hunted scowl. She was aggressively impatient and unforthcoming with the press, and *German* to boot. At the mention of her name it was mandatory to fill the new Wembley Arena with louts and old ladies so they could chant in unison...

More to her than meets the eye!

Well the clever old *Sun* had been asking around the Maths department about her. She had no friends who

---

[95] The 3-year-old daughter of Kate and Gerry McCann who was abducted on a family holiday in the Algarve. Kate was referenced earlier in the report of the WI reading.

were not in cyberspace, so it had to be colleagues. Well, they seem to have got Neil Stebbing drunk over a 'slap-up' dinner in *The Ubiquitous Chip*[96] leading the socially challenged mathematical logician to let loose some facts and thoughts. That Sabbine used to refer to Nobby as 'the retard' and that she said she sometimes felt like chaining him up in the cellar (this was the best she could manage in terms of irony). Then we get to Neil's little theory, as brandy chased desert wine, and almost certainly articulated with the prosody of lines of Lisp[97] multiply-embedded and negated: "It is not implausible that Dr. Stripentau could conceivable not have been not guilty of the murder of young Norbert. She did not not lack a long fuse when it came to elements in her life that were not not intractable and which did not not not lack intellectual brilliance." Something along those lines, I'd imagine.

Let me see now, not (not(not possess))... never mind. This was translated by the *The Sun* as "Top boffin says Sab killed Nob."

Then the lucky old *Sun* probably went round to Bantock Avenue and told one or two the neighbours what Stebbing had 'said'. Somebody reported she had seen Sabbine smacking Nobby's legs when he did his stick-body act against being strapped into the back seat of her SUV. And her semi-detached neighbour said he's heard through the wall "Just leave me alone, Nobby, and learn some independence. Scheisser!" A loud bump, and then "I'll run you over with my exercise bike and squash you like a little

---

[96] An upmarket restaurant in Byres Road Glasgow (see note 2).

[97] A computer programming language.

fuckeen hedgehowg." There's that irrepressible GSOH again, of which she spoke so often on her many dating profiles.

But how then did the silly old *Sun* square this with the refractory datum that I had run away. Easily done. "It was generally believed that Craigie was under the spell of the German and would do anything for her... He was hypnotized by love, as by a snake," a friend of the couple "said." "He must have fled to deflect [yes, that word in *The Sun*!] the blame from her."

We had no friends in common. This was clearly a fantasy friend of the novelist *manqué* who wrote the piece. In fact, I used to refer to Sabbine to friends as Andromeda[98], mimicking her Spock-like utterances... "Erna is crying in her room, which makes me sink she is upset right now"... "I could not sleep last night from sinking about the real numbers seminar." She was my butt. (Hi there, Modrick old mate!)

The idea was, then, that I had shot off as a scapegoat.

Later editions of *The Mirror* and the *The Mail* carried the 'story'.

Idiots might think this was good news for me. What overrode the bollocks was the fact – as they went on to detail with relish – that she was now 'neglecting her children' to pursue an 'obsessive' relationship with The Toilet. They

---

[98] This is a reference to the early-'60s TV series called *A for Andromeda* about a girl (straight blonde hair, robotic, yet played by Julie Christie) who was assembled on earth by computerised instructions from another planet.

went away for 'mini-breaks' in 'castles' by lochs. They queued for rock gigs and night-clubs. And here she was getting out of his car dressed like every young man's fantasy. This was a disaster. No, I did not jump into a vat of *Butcombes* coming up only for *Paddy* chasers.

I take disaster neat. I walked inland, and had a filthy lunch in a back-street café called *The Lemon Tree*, most of the time being the only customer, reading through all my newspapers. I inverted reality and imagined the place as a hot meeting point in the early '60s – *Expresso Bongo*[99], Johnny Dankworth, Lionel Bart, the clean-cut cod-Americana with Italian scooters, plastic tomatoes of red sauce, Chianti bottles in baskets, stocking tops, heavy petting. I drafted a poem on the back of the advertising fliers from my tabloids – number 32. It turned out to reflect the means-end life and the question of what to say and do when you pause in the sequence. All my habits are there: half-buried sources (in rough order) – B. Dylan, Dylan, T. (spat out in a Fitzrovia pub), Ashbery (almost) and Eliot (at the end), with a Stevens borrowing (the horse in the breast) for good measure. Not to mention the clodhoppingly obvious Goethe (*Kennst du das Land...*) re the lemons. It's actually preaching in pre-sleep language, with some Hugo Williams nostalgia and sub, sub-Ashbery for still more measure. Oh, and my addiction to coining proper names. Writing it helped. Drink would have helped more, maybe...

---

[99] A musical of the period, written by Wolf Mancovitz. Cliff Richard and Lawrence Harvey starred in the movie.

32: The Lemon Tree

Life & life only to float through transom
catalyst of skim, in black polo neck
and Levi's, cleave to the
coffee bar cowboys, ss-ss steam heat

into freeze frame. Such sittings &
sippings sculpt Hepworth holes in
which the mind moves as fox-snout –
the galloping horse in the breast, the
clip-clop secretary at 7am in the
breast an equestrian statue now.

***

The Lemon Tree, The Bootsie Bar, chin-
music jukes, jazz at the Tick-Tock , folk
at the Lady of Même, emptied
home. Forty-two years of this with
content thinning, "like hair" says Malc.

***

The gang's all here to baby death
resigned. Speak! "Still-born little
couple" in 42"-waist jeans.
    We held cloud network
narrative, trip series in squirrel
garden, not acting but habiting,
movement sans desire, desire as
drill, sequelae run to zero. As
    Malc said the boots he

James Russell

polishes at dawn by a cold radiator
out of sight
    of the sea — Do you
know that land? — yet soft words
in his throat above a creaking belt
warm and sincere.

***

Tick tock, rum baba's off. He lies
in a bath, radio in steam, sees
the grey CD ring as sky scape. What
next? To catch a train? See lager-pumped youth
settle to periodicals and fruit?

1st November, 2007

Since that day all my dreams – there have been many – have been about people from my distant past. Last night about Roy Maine. Six feet four inches of pure intellect roiled by lust, and now a Professor of middle eastern studies at Yale. My best friend at Oxford. We had met for drinks a few times since then but I didn't really enjoy them. The drink would start well, with talk about women and who is now doing what, but eventually the engine would fill up with the sand of his primary obsession (even before what he came to call 'pussy'). This was Avicenna's[100] 'floating man' argument. It's essentially a thought experiment in which Avicenna imagines a man, with eyes and ears blocked from input, floating, splayed like a starfish a few feet above the earth, so there can be no tactual or kinaesthetic (is it?) input. But – are you following me now!? – he is still a mental entity... so the mind can (what?) be experienced without the body. A big load of nothing to my mind; but Roy was wanting to explain to me (why?) how it could be improved as to establish more than Descartes' *cogito*. I merely think now of the floating man as Donald Crowhurst[101], the poor floating sod. And I thought too (going back to the Roy era) of our sitting

---

[100] Ibn Sina, Abu 'Ali al-Husayn (980–1037), a famously lustful and bibulous Muslim scholar who lived in what is now Iran.

[101] Crowhurst took part in the *Sunday Times* round-the-world race in 1968 in a boat that was ill-prepared. He made radio silence and sat it out on the coast of Brazil, omitting The Horn and catching up with the leaders. He would have come third, but he could not sustain the deception and committed suicide.

through Strawson[102] on Kant... So here were my mud pie thoughts on the necessity for being an agent in a refractory world if there is to be a mind. So that was number 33. Fair cop, nicked prosody and lay-out, loosely, from a poem in *Wound Response*[103].

---

[102] The late Sir Peter Strawson, one time Professor of Metaphysics at Oxford – a neo-Kantian.

[103] A collection by J.H. Prynne, published in 1974.

33: The Floating Man

The sea camber falls flat beneath his acts
of spray, not making its point, some wind brings
data to him
                              pendant in raw feel,
up for grabs, by the tourist boat proving
radio presence. Look mate,
there's a lovely pressure as the somnam-
bulist's cogito makes grist for the panders
who shrink from these neurotrash sops; blind
drunk all the way to the skip. His nous
bright but encumbered. The milk of conflation
licks over sensorium quite short.
For pickling the head with doubt his blank
modus drives the point inward, all
atrophied white from thinking.
                          This show will
explode myths, each peasant's lips soon
start shredding all ingrate. His hands flap free
                as feathers on an oily spitting Aga.
                He floats a
                thoughtframe cloud chamber.
Properties are washing out, now that touch
is no meal in this gruel of mulch,
to synthesise all pucka aspect;
his home is Teignmouth, his kids are
blinking to horizon trained. Crowds
raise funds in council house cook outs, while
the strophe commands his piss-poor pen-bites.
All the planning in salt & wife & camera
gives the lie-in-life a soft housing
on a smear of brie.

James Russell

This is the body whose sway lets in
the sunlight of blue & red convergence.
Why float a heaven off shore?
       Confirmation
that this heaven's a minus sign?
He's convinced he's sanctioned all data about him,
frictionless prophylactic movements centre
      on a selfish hair-lipped grin
      no luscious thrall
to our anchoring stuff.
      Now he's back
by the lie annealed
      bold as air
and half as solid,
      but this pink shell-fish
is comfortably no combatant
      nor shining mental conjunct;
      see gut-ropes now slip
      free, the waves caress
      and now his feet
feel the kiss of cod scales and green plankton.
This agent folds up pre-drowned & a hero.

5th November, 2007

I'm losing my taste for things, living exhausted in the dream of a life. Nothing impinges on me now, certainly not the miseries of others. To wit, Shine's. It turns out that the reason Shine's here is that his wife of nearly forty years has been fading away in a 'home' in Nailsea, too ill to be moved. That's where he goes during the day. She died two or these days ago.

He's been going around the place since then with a face fixed in a glassy smile. The smile is a tourniquet against tears. As when I invited him up for a drink after supper yesterday it relaxed itself till he sat on my pouffe reminiscing without sense – and blubbering. I felt it was more or less expected of me to achieve some physical contact at this point so I got down from the bed and put an arm round his shoulder. I may even have said something like "Let it all out, Phil, that's the way." And would have meant "...so you're empty enough to bugger off back to your own room." I wondered how long I should hold the position. I broke it after about a minute, moved back to the bed, but shortly after felt a guilt pang about my distance from the old boy. This kept happening. In all, I must have got down from the bed to re-engage him about ten times, on each occasion returning because my calves hurt. It must have looked like we were rehearsing a scene in a play we couldn't get right. I felt nothing beyond a vague boredom; not even socially located enough to be embarrassed.

But when he finally rose to leave – he had even missed *Newsnight* – he clamped me in surprisingly strong arms, squeezing my breath away. I did my best to reciprocate, feeling all the time as if it was he comforting *me*. "Thank you, Duncan. Thank you, Duncan. You're a good man." He left and it was my turn now. This was not like the Long Ashton 'biting-the-air' collapse, but was rather the sudden genuflecting surrender to the central fact of an un-central man: that I am a worthless creature, utterly alone, and actually about five years old. [*Och! Yoooure nae hard tae mistake furr a ray o'sunshine, so yoooure not, Moira.*]

6th November 2007

"Of course, the police will never take any of this seriously" was what I was telling myself. But when Christoph, Sabbine's ex-husband, decided to get in on the act, they did so, to the extent of there being talk of fresh DNA tests. Let me explain[104]. Sabbine had left me in the house that Saturday morning with Nobby – me in bed reading the paper wearing my headphones and him playing with his collection of toy cars – while she ferried the girls round to their father's. (There they would usually spend a comparatively normal day, for a change, baking with Christoph's girlfriend.) Well, Christoph had thought again, bent over the *Sun* or his theorems, about the 'fateful morning', and had re-interrogated his visual image of Sabbine's SUV standing in his drive. Originally, Nobby was not there, but when he came to *think* about it... he was "60-70% certain" he saw the boy's feet, wearing his favourite dog-face slippers, kicking up at the back window. So this meant that JC never had that 'fateful window of opportunity to do the deed' – *The Mirror* had to manage a pun on 'window' somehow. Apparently, either we did it together or she did it alone after I had gone home.

Yup! A man's godda do... etc. In this case stand by and see Sabbine tortured afresh. See the old wounds ripped open and some new ones added just for her, see her sexual history spread across the *News of the World* (pages 7-12, with pictures), see her referred to in *The Mail* as The Toilet's 'mistress', see her psychologised and sociologised by

---

[104] But explain to whom? [Quite so, Claire mate. Cheers. Ed.]

some unqualified woman idiot in the *Guardian G2*, see her tearful rage before the intrusive lenses.

I find that at the worst moments, clichés get painted in fresh colours: It *doesn't bear thinking about.* No, it does not.

7th November, 2007

I suppose the word is 'inanition': literally exhausted, *qua* mentally spent. I posited a *Joy Division* track today, from an imaginary CD of theirs, called *Inanition. Doyning diddy, doyning diddy, boom doyning IN-AN-I-SHUN!* I've been going around singing it. This is what the Sabbina – in fact of Sabbina *and Toilet* – news has done to me.

I don't know what's cause and what's effect here but I'm not sleeping properly since my *Sun*-day. I am in bed for hours and most of the time I'm not fully awake; but I'm not sleeping either. That's to say, I dream about my project of getting back to sleep. A blues band shares my bed (middle aged balding men in rugby shirts and executive voices) who promise they will not practice too loud; Red Indians (in dreams begin un-PC-abilities[105]) camping on the Thames Barrier advise me to turn over and mutter nonsense to myself, which I then do; then I cuddle myself into a ball in an Easyjet queue while Hugh Paddick[106] and Frank Dacey[107] toss coins for who will tell me that I'm about to wake up. Which I do. To stare at the whitening curtains till it's time to get up, two hours later.

But strangest of all, I've lost my taste for booze again, but seriously so this time; while the glutton project is now an

---

[105] Almost certainly a nod to Delmore Schwartz's well-known story *In Dreams begin Responsibilties*.

[106] A comic actor best known for his work with Kenneth Williams on *Round the Horn* and *Beyond our Ken*.

[107] A school friend, now a New York divorce lawyer.

impossible dream. The Paddy bottle gathers dust. Now, if I try to drink beer it seems to me like something between molasses and gravy. If I force something alcoholic down my gullet (G&Ts the least bad), I don't get drunk – just tired, rattish and queasy. I could not eat a fun-sized[108] *Mars Bar* if you paid me (note the clever use of cliché here). Of course, I'm losing weight. I don't have the will to shave my face let alone my head, so the result is that I look like a Buddhist monk who, after having had a bag of flour tipped over his head, has dipped his face in a basin of water.

I go for walks. Now instead of meandering up to the *Salthouse* I swerve

---

[108] This is, 'small'.

34: The Belle Balloon

Rising proud, skirting the clouds, Big Belle
the First, lets out some slack in
real sunshine. Long spent on nascent curve
from all known wantons of wind.
    Silver froth blowing free;
    the bright eye; blue crowning
    the swell, rolling with wrack –
the kidney of pathos, and the
old heart, beating for removal and rest.
South West to sea, is the source
of a different light made from darkly
    sculpted & nurtured inanition:
    it enchants us, sleeping confirmed
    in our embroiling folds. But love
sinks to its knees, now exhausted in
mentation frame, as it breathes a whiff
of continental rot. That light
    sanctions all the cruél burrs
    swaying in frondy minds; & we cop
    its phobic blasts with shrugging eyes.
Such patches from imbruing. Such thoughts form
inferno proud while the stains are dark and shining.
My mavens have grown wings and flown inland,
leaving a drenched statue without loss,
saying there has been sufficient shivering by bar codes:
    the smooth horizon calls, & the
    lovely mantua of cloud-scrap is
    too far up, hedged out of mind.
Listen now: henceforth no *mare clausum*, &
mare librum lives inland. To walk a seam
well stitched with history is one way, or to

lie regressive in a pool of bile. On
either path that farther light will shine
    until my world moves south &
    west and I cry for paradox & beer
    laughing in my own face. The
inferno that I spoke of, the inanition, are
my closest friends. That self-styled 'taste
of freedom': Is stomach acid on the
tongue? As sweet as summer dew?
No bootless garlanding in off-the-peg
bon-bons; I have spent so far
only fish scales in this watery frame.

past it with a martial stride, making for the coastal path. As I walk I ponder what I could safely do to help Sabbine. Take a day-return to some distant city and post a letter to the Glasgow police saying I acted alone? Then of course those in the grip of the theory that I'm a love-sick donkey will merely say "Well, he would, wouldn't he?" But mostly what I want to do is to write to Sabbine and tell her that The Toilet will destroy her and that I still love her. In which case she would tell nobody about the letter and file in under 'Craigie, J. – varia' in her neat office.

Got soaked to the skin this afternoon on the coastal path, but I didn't care because I was watching a blue-and-white dirigible flying past – a gorgeous sight, and a bizarre one at this time of the year. As this was happening, something shifted inside of me. I couldn't quite say what, but it was about feeling myself placed in relation to all the good and all the bad in the world. I did not think that what I had done was not so bad in relation to the really bad stuff

– give me credit – but I felt like a citizen among events and objects. I was almost in the role of Coleridge's water-snakes[109]: poisonously one of God's creatures.

Actually, number 34 did not really turn out to address that; though there are shades of it deeper than a slag mine[110]. As I walked home I felt at peace, hungry and ready for a drink. I kick-started the poem with an armature taken from Prynne's *The Western Gate*. But now I am putting these props away, placing Prynne's brick of cosmic custard[111] at the bottom of the pile. No more painting by numbers. Arise Sir Jack from Prynne's procrustean prosody bed! As the *Stones* did not sing:

I'm constrained!
to do what I want
any old time.

And now I wonder: why have I finished two Prynnishes with reference to fish scales? An unconscious echo of feeble armour with a pun on 'amour', I would say, Terry.

---

[109] Craigie is referring to a scene in *The Rime of the Ancient Mariner*.

[110] This is 'inspired' by a line from John Cooper Clarke's *Thirty-six hours*: 'Shades of doubt go deeper than a slag mine'.

[111] This was a phrase used by Iain Sinclair in a discussion of JHP in Radio 3. Prynne's collected poems is a large yellow book.

9th November, 2007

As I was burying Prynne's collected among my other books – though not (be reverend! as we used to say age seven) too deeply – I happened upon a book I hadn't opened for about thirty five years – Jonathan Raban's *The Society of the Poem*, Harrap, 1971 and '£1.00 net'. Flooding nostalgia and the boogie woogie blues. (You can tell I'm getting better, can't you, chuck!). Cover: dark brown, orange, and cream (not a combination unknown in the early '70s).

I had bought it because, in my Islington years, I'd lived upstairs from the author. In 1970 he occupied the basement flat of an Arundel Square house, and I lived upstairs with a bunch of fellow postgrads, a post-doc or two, a drop-out from a Physics Ph.D. at Cambridge (a sick-makingly arrogant South African who sponged off his girlfriend and had written more hilarious 'poems' than he had read), and later some freeloading pseudo-hippy creeps [*Calm down, Moira, and drink yooour tea!]* from North America. JR was friendly, and even invited us all to a party in the early days, at which I recall a bath-full of ice cubes and white wine bottles. My lingering image of him is his trying to get a deceased MG Midget started, bought from the Rasta-run garage nearby. A tall, academically long-haired (no need for baseball caps in those days) young man in a blue-velvet suit was cajoling some skins into pushing it... "Do you think you could possibly..."

We never had a one-to-one conversation, but I liked him. For one thing, he was a gentleman. F'rinstance... One of the pseudo-hippy creeps (a Canadian who called himself

'Crash') had a great, snorting motor-bike which he would rev in the small hours right by Jonathan's bedroom window. Also, the creeps found it a truly groovy way of announcing to anybody in the kitchen that – hey, you guys! – they had reached the ground floor was to jump the last four stars onto the bare-wood passageway. This, it turned out, thundered directly above his sleeping head. To cover both matters, Jonathan wrote us a letter, in a beautiful italic hand, beginning more or less "It goes against the grain for me to write to neighbours with grumbles like this, but..."

The Californian hippy – think Frank Zappa crossed with a young Philip Roth – reacted to this, predictably enough, with "Well, he can just go fuck himself." Now here was a man difficult to admire. I shall never forget his description of the landlord's nice but eager-to-please wife as 'Clarissa Cold Cunt'. In fact, this was a man who, in a just world, would at this time in his life have been having flesh-eating ants folded into his eye-sockets by the Viet Cong. [*Och, Moira pleeease! People are watching.*]

Anyway (if this diary is ever published it should be called 'Anyway'), back to the book, the book which he must have been writing as I was puffing cigars upstairs and growing my big black beard (no, no, not at all like Marx!). It is excellent – measured, elegantly-written, and lucid. I will recommend it to my final-year undergraduates, and indeed it could be opened with profit by the general reader, always bearing in mind that the only way I'll get my name onto a dusk jacket is by writing an arse-licking puff for it.

One thing stayed behind about the book, in an early chapter about socio-political poems. JR quoted in full a poem recently published in *Tribune* in response to the Bangladeshi flood of 1971. It was probably heartfelt, and it was certainly bad. It was not, in any sense, poetic; but was rather a bit of reportage wrapped around in poesy scarves. What had struck me at the time about it, and what struck, or wetly swatted, me now was the *exhaustion* it expressed. Each phrase was like a painful step homeward, planted by puppet legs. Even bad writing can be enjoyable if it has energy. I don't mean linguistic energy. I just mean the everyday stuff that pulls us up to dance or makes us run for a bus. Kerouac and K. Amis had little linguistic energy but plenty of the latter kind, so their work could be a good read. But this stuff. Stroll on! This lead to number 35. OK, I felt like the school bully's winger reading it through but, well... you know.

35: Tender is the Shite[112]

*The living picked their way, silently,
among the dead, looking ahead.
Stillness was imaged at their feet,
shrugged overhead like a kite.*
Darkness fell for two hours in dust
over taxi-door ears constrained
in tight caps. Democracy meanwhile creaked
like a hinge, one from oil estranged,
till doomsday and the iron-monger's cry:
"No one's too young or too old to die!"
Stone me! *The very corpses seem awake
lollying in mud with sucking lips
as if their thirsts to slake.*

In the air nothing;
birds swooped and clawed everywhere.
What else was there for them to do
now that the shells had flown
like budget flights to eternity?
We'll spill the contents of fate's cup.
*Some long thin hair, a cravat,
and a hare sitting up
will be all that's left.*
Shit   I give up.

---

[112] Lines from the original poem are in italics.

Shortly after I finished this Jason knocked. He said he has some "intriguing intelligence to convey" (this was a lovely example of 6th-form arch). Being his usual helpful self and scanning the internet for Prynnish events, he had come across a 'Cambridge Evening' at Bristol University's poetry society, being held in two days' time. Yep, this would do for me. The main event was a reading by Grantin Storn'way of his latest pamphlet *Sieve Marty Song*. To explain, Strorn'way is the big cat among the new generation of Prynnites, did his Ph.D. on Prynne, supervised by... Prynne. Something of the rock star about his reputation. I'd already heard him read thanks to a download from Jason – a live performance of a furiously-paced whirl of martial arts poesy called *Staple Sex For*. The audience loved it, his voice a bone-dry cheeky chappie. Jason said that unfortunately he couldn't come with me as he had a rehearsal for *Black Comedy* that night.

13th November, 2007

Caught the bus at Six Ways, feeling like a spy setting off to recce a building. A strange excitement swelled as the bus bashed through the overhanging branches into Bristol and swelled some more as I puffed my way up Park Street to the venue. It was not so much that I knew I would enjoy it: it was this all right, but tinged with the thought that if I did not then the Prynnish project might not thrive. Daft, of course.

I was a bit late and caught the tail-end of the second reading – just in time for the interval after which Storn'way would appear. My first impression of the present reader was that of a starved boy who had been kept in a box-room all of his life by parents who thought it was still 1938. He had been fed on bread-and-dripping and educated from *The Children's Encyclopaedia*. When he looked up from his text his big black eyes were seemingly in terror and then they darted back to it like beetles to a skirting-board. What's more, he would stutter in spasms at certain points... And then I woke up. First these were not stutters but poetic moves. No doubt they were written something like this:

>   *Your cr I mean*
>   *crossed be*
>   *beauty   entire*
>   *ly front this bee   this*
>   *beach.*

It was not fear in his eyes but intensity. Also, his clothes and hair (as if he were a painting by L.S. Lowry called

Thin Boy) were carefully studied. A flimsy white shirt (though the weather was freezing) and a liquorice-string tie, his black hair worn short-back-and-sides and hitlered over his brow, and, the masterstoke – grey flannels held up with thin brown braces. He was still an undergraduate. His poem? Probably interesting, but, frankly, I wasn't really listening.

I queued up for my free thimble of wine and paid £3 for Storn'way's pamphlet (beautifully produced). I sat sipping and reading, my expectations sinking somewhat; so I stopped reading. In the text there were arrows, there were broken words, there were bullet points and #s and asterisks, rivulets of semi-sense, phrases cut from other discourses and welded onto a doubtless-strong but non-human-seeming trestle. Best to leave it for now.

I was pretty sure I knew which one he was. People approached the guy and in giving each polite attention he would frequently rear up like a horse, not at something they had said, I suspect, but in order to protect them from the pungent impact of his own utterance. He had the nervous energy and electric self-consciousness of one who is about to perform, and who knows there is much expected of him.

Yes it was him all right. Grantin Storn'way. I was put in mind of middle-period Peter Sellars, a young Harold Pinter and – God help us – a young Jonathan King. [*Och, why not a teenage Kenny McKellar, Moira!*] A strange tension between his smooth, happy-to-please preamble to the poem and the introduction he had been given by a pleasing girl. She said – the mood was light – that the principal concerns of his verse were "blow-jobs, anal sex, and neo-cons" and that the work was, in a nutshell, "an enormous fuck-you." I would like, if I may, to make two points here Chairman. First, how ironic that Larkin, who surely (OK, possibly) inspired the 'an enormous [ejaculation]' formula[113], is a figure much despised surely (or possibly) within the 'Cambridge School'. Second, the work is anything *but* an enormous fuck-you. And those who think it is would certainly (yes) trot out phrases to describe it like 'a punk sensibility' or a 'punk energy'. In fact, what one gets is not nihilism but a scattergun intelligence from an abstract, obsessive, politically-literate source. Not fuck-you then, but as much to-audience sensitivity as that of a new lecturer to his first class. He aims to pull you in, to make his point, to do the job. And while the performance would not have raised an eyebrow a little under 100 years ago in a Zurich cabaret, the target is not the bourgeoisie and their fur-lined world of 'Art' but our unconsciousness of the modern world – of global politics. He is also a drowning-in-irony love poet.

The Martin Song of the title was at once a piece of internet flotsam and the shape of things to come. The theme (in the sense of Churchill's "this pudding" having or lacking "a theme") was China, and its burgeoning potential for saying an 'enormous fuck-you' to the West. The modus operandi was familiar: you make poetry from the raw data banging up against the contemporary sensorium, at the stage before they reach the synthesising mind. It is not allowed *near* the poet's synthesising mind, so if you

---

[113] In his poem *For Sydney Bechet*, which contains the lines 'On me your voice falls as they say love should,/Like an enormous yes.'

want synthesis you can do it yourself, m'dear, with one or two pointers from him. I had been exposed to this kind of thing before – delighted by it – in the work of Tony Lopez; but this was an entirely different kettle.

On the downside... I remember reading a review of one of a Roger McGough collection in the *TLS* in the late '60s in which the anonymous reviewer ended by saying "You can almost hear the birds in the front row giggling." Elements of that here. Second, the long poem – it took about forty minutes to read – evoked the internet in ways surely or possibly not intended: the deliberately incoherent English of spam emails about Viagra or penis extensions, with their clusters of top-row keyboard symbols. Relatedly, the performance held the attention, but the content often did not. I wanted more and broader jokes. The mind of ol' Jack Craigie wandered often to the question of what Sabbine and The Toilet were doing at that exact moment. I recalled the gentle poison she had poured into my ear about former lovers. The Toilet's ears may be singeing his hair now.

But, all-in-all, I loved it. My faith was re-booted and re-upholstered and given a bottle of *Pol Roger* by Lord Boothby. I found myself smiling, surprising myself in shop windows and in the black windows of the Clevedon bus. Some yobs got on when it stopped outside the chip-shop in Long Ashton, and they started to throw their chips at me. But I was such that I found myself catching and eating them and announcing in my best podium-trained voice: "More please, lads. I'm starvin', me."

17th November, 2007

You might say it's been a good couple of days for me; though if you did, Lord knows where you would have been sitting. Certainly, my old appetites and energy made a comeback. Here again was the blinkered optimism more usually associated with the duffer-by-principle. Thus, my dutiful passion for what is meaty and beaty in music took me by the hand a led me as far as... *Girls Aloud*[114].

Last night I woke up at 2am with one of the numbers from their latest CD recursing in my mind with industrial strength; and in the morning I found myself mouthing it:

> *I can't speak French*
> *So I let the funky music*
> *Do the talkin' talkin' now*

I was addicted to the *talkin' talkin'* and relished the parallel to

> *The way that you walK*
> *The way that you talK*
> *[inaudible, rhymes with 'ocK]*

from a track on their previous CD. You know, I would bet good money, Dr. Maliphant, that these lines were sung by the same young lady.

---

[114] Recently judged by *The Guinness Book of Records* to be the best selling girl group of all time.

And it was in this mood that I wrote number 36. All done in one day. Clocked in at 8 am; clocked out at 11 pm. It was intended, and started out as a half-hearted imitation of Storn'way, of course; but it changed into a kind of low-key, subjective mish-mash. I mean low-key relative to ol' Grantin. Political in my own little way: the cathedral/mosque in Corboba[115], *The Song of Roland*[116], and my current reading of *Palestinian Walks*[117] by Raja Shehadeh (a sad, lovely book). We are, after all, living within the new Crusades, while the debasement-by-rendering-punctate of Palestinians in their own country is now just about the only global issue that heats my blood. Well... others do too of course; but this I feel as a personal affront — the slow, cleverly calculated, inexorable bullying, yes *bullying* Mr Bob Dylan[118]! "It's yours now I suppose, but what does 'yours' mean in this complex world? And it did *used* to be mine. OK, three thousand years ago; but need I even mention by *divine right*. So I think we had better call it mine now, don't you old son. And let's not hear anything about your *suffering* shall we. You don't

---

[115] Corboba was the capital of Andalusia –– Moorish Spain. On this site there was originally a Christian temple (to St. Vincent). The construction of the mosque was begun in 785. Corboba was re-conquered by the Christians in 1236. A Cathedral was build in the centre of the mosque during the 16th Century.

[116] A narrative poem of unknown authorship written in French in the 11th century. It describes events, or an elision of events, that took place about 300 years earlier namely a battle between Charlemagne's Frankish army and the Muslims of northern Spain, and its aftermath.

[117] Profile Books, 2007. The author, a Palestinian Lawyer, describes how Jewish settlements and concrete are destroying the landscape around his native Ramallah, and insidiously eroding the Palestinian forms of life.

[118] Craigie will be thinking here of Dylan's Israel-defending number *Neighbourhood Bully*, from the album *Infidels*.

know the meaning of the word, now do you old chum. Eh? Eh?" OK, my mind goes all Pinterish at this point. You can see why all Pinter's artistry and humour goes phutt when faced with state-orginated bullying[119]. A sentence comes to mind like a volley of punches; but when you write it down – limp as Lois.

So I put these bits in a blender, but only pressed the button for 200 milliseconds; so there are gobbets sound enough for me to sidle, snigger and curlicue among. Some cruel people might call this knitting vomit. Of *course* they do.

You've guessed it. I detest laptops. But I borrowed Jason's to do this one, needing font-range and a symbol-kitty. Printed it off and left it on the Brother as per.

---

[119] See the entry for 26th December.

James Russell

36: Ken Medina BSc

∞ KENNETH ROAD, LUTON UK ∞

• The sky that thinks it's a screen-saver
• The fountain pen that thinks it's a tooth-pick
The informational encapsulation of force meat & night soil
• The mosque that thinks it's a cathedral

He noticed the severe of the yawn full in the
thin sun.

⇒ Don't pick up dropped coins from the floor &
nod agreement with a sentence at the same time/don't test the acoustics of the holy building at floor level by means of head dipping

The Basilican structure is characteristic of
money well spent.

∞ max approval to cervza-sipping/to jamón-chomping in this building.
Oh we'll give you a kiss with tongues 'neath the triumphalist
shit in the capilla ∞

⇒ Don't test the resilience of the floor slabs with your forehead. Don't Ken, no Kenny NO.

Seek the rationality of the orgone box beetle-stuffed with genetic epistemology, then you can deny the weather-beaten old employees with their sprigs of lucky heather, walk like Charlemagne, be-scarved against the air, while the emir said to give

some thought to deciding to repent my actions towards him; I
had slain his son & I knew bang right my challenge to his country
was unjust.

My love she is a working girl
    with maraschino sores.
Her penis is the size of a big broad
    bean, but she is full of cares.
Her phatic speech shines like a
    fang, form fang, slap fang; stop.
She spends her days on the IN TER
    NET a'searching for a love, they come/
they go. They leave her raw as beans
    grow in the field.

'Love' biconditionally implies Kennetta Medina who speaks:
"Oh come and climb to know the REAL Dave Cameron. Simp-
lamente a bleached Maya Angelou with
an infantile vulva, now at the lower rate/
inspect the value of your fuck-up.

This Medina, this kiss-curl on temple shine:
She is no symbol nor concept even
rather she is a something that depends
upon no properties; she determines
no properties. She is free-
range meat –
made of properties that instantiate
only themselves; as B. Russell
showed in effect to assume otherwise
is to invite contradiction. Oh
Lord these puss-white indigenous
Lutons freely shoot at her and spill

her water when she rambles between
the bus station and Luton's own
Arndale Centre, finding like love
crocuses between pavement cracks.

Like a thought-wracked Alma
Cogan she sculpts herself around
Build a Settlement, Create a Fact (this
is not a Girls Aloud number) around
a life where every baby wears neat
blue button-down shirts & pork pie
suits & Christmas joy always sums
to 180^0. Her mind as an unvisited
red & yellow throbbing disco on
the Liverpool-Belfast ferry full of
Eastern promises.

   All this one may write in a
real bed, less said the dimmer till
   gross-point nurture cleaves
mental in the cross-charnel disco.

   You pull back in mind when
he steps forth as Ken Medina BSc
   pock-marked drum-boy of floor
sweat, lease holder of his butch swagger

   And torn lobes, English as
the click of leather on damp skin.
   You pull forward in body when
Ken drops his glass sword and swigs Rust

Brew in Café Noire. Then m'dear
the entree fades as smoke across
Ken's temples throb to the news:
Paien unt tort e chrestïens unt dreit[120]

Some news is bad news patient
as a blue bike leaning on a fence
he picks a fight with himself bee-
soft and rippling with honey muscle.

There is an airport on a hill dominating
the water supply of Lower Luton
hard by the crisp stall is the home
in which a skilled operator twists tendons
till the truth will out
his left lobe = skinned-rabbit Fred
short back and front, worried scowl;
his right lobe = Bert Troutman
communist wearer of the polo neck.
His home is now covered with
pure snow like white honey.
To say
he is merely 'cruel' is as to
confuse his rubber blood bucket
with Saint Jerome.

∞ KENNETH MONJOIE ∞

Baffled hard-off free style, full English
in the cloister. Crack on! Crack on!
She is rejoicing in the ugly nineteenth

---

[120] The pagans are wrong and the Christians are right. (Old French)

century stained glass. Chrestïene est par
veire conoisance[121]

Her reality TV idea is widely adopted now:
Hey Jude! = A collusion between the boy-friend
& Channel Clive. He stands her up
in a bower of hidden cameras. A Jude Law
lookie-likee – or Jude Law – turns up instead.
He and millions watch as she decides re
the surrogate. A falcon drops upon
a field mouse. Capiche?

        On a planted plane resentment grows
   some people are free at every point, lean rifles
           turn on, sea bathed now in oil
    they move their limbs & a white crust falls.

        Daddy, daddy, what is "tea-bagging"? You
pull forward in body when Ken does
      nothing, when he is patient & unknown
You pull away in mind when he aims split-peas

        At a tea-ball. When he says at lunch
"Odi et amo" you say "Yeah, right, Sid Caesar"
      In Pancho hats and codicils the big enthrals.
Satan too is standing there putting on his

        Act. Who is painting chevrons in my path"
I am said Satan, his downy cheeks drawing your
        own face from the constricted stones making
friends with a virtuoso mime – as if Jim

---

[121] She is a Christian, convinced of the truth. (Old French)

Medina should rhyme 'tripe' with 'cellotape'
affronts us all. The arse-cream man finite and foregone
with painful-to-read conjectures all fried in
gesture. You miss the pulled-away mind and sea body.

Mauve in his Christmas sweater, Ken
tries his amber-and-gold-inlaid sword for sharp.
Nothing comes quite to mind.
His neighbours teeth are on the floor, brains
too & nasals slit by Nordomile
The King of Swords. Through
the neighbour's buttocks, clean between
& through the wooden floor of strong wood
lodged now in a conduit for water — refreshment
washes the turkey pap and sex-pink delight away.
"You [he speaks] are a Pole from Poland. Not
short but neither are you tall, keen eyes you
have and broad of neck you and white of beard.
Your mower now rusts in my shed
Oh vile worshipper of what'shisface."

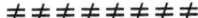

Egregiously well-informed with a Rolls Royce
orbito-frontal region Professor Kenneth Monjoie!
inspects himself promising hand-on-hip to
be true to his own vision of mordancy.

Coddle the setting between chiaroscuro &
tuck-shop, coddle the setting my boy twixt
camphor and sapphire, coddle the
leitmotiv coddle the depth, but this pulling

Away in mind Prof M. abhors in itself
in her, stuck at home drunk on benefits
selling rainwater, distrusted by her patients
bathed in pink light & Dead Sea sweat

She keeps pickled walnuts in her money
belt, capons in her priest-hole, pretty dear
pretty pretty-ugly woman with your frightened
scowl, your acne and your backing off welcome
to the night – welcome to the food chain.

∞ KENNETH PRIM AGITATION ∞

'Deus,' dist li reis, 'si penuse est ma vie!'[122]

There are options: early withdrawal but with less, unimaginative pushing on in body with the mind moving as far back as the baggage cars, ripe for ambush from the hills – my one or two ideas dying heroically with blood exploding from their temples. (I think of something novel, it blows its own trumpet – then expires.) If I withdraw, my mind will stay mine. I'll join a gym pumping steel with old ladies/swimming with pre-schoolers, eat only pub food, get to know the other Withdrawns in the Open-All-Days. I'll try internet-dating… "Charles". I am very brave, or so my friends tell me! Unique sense of humour.

There is no sense of achievement, except to have got away with it. They had to obey, but they found themselves free to slag me off to my face. Anything – I tell you – for a night with Juliana.

---

[122] 'God', said the king, 'how wearisome my life is!' (Old French)

Lust fails to fall away with the whitening of the beard. Of course, it could be achieved by power assertion, but she would be far back in mind; and what use is that to me?

To have my orders carried out was like writing words on a blank page. But what of word order? Orders come to mind, and there they stand in rank. Having obeyed, the words look up and tell me off. If this is the free action of the Supervisory System, you can keep it.

•••Bleach! Someone has thrown it at the sky.
It's taken the colour from my Activating System.
A cursory look at selected development
indicators (Table 3a) shows a smile
dryin up little by little my tryin
to figure out what's goin on inside
her head. You got any idea how
I feel? Plotting
a research tool as organs
work together to form systems, Reticular
Systems. I have people to poke or kick
mine and so I wake to this sopping
white sky. I wanted one svelte &
compelling & now have this: 24 bases
of which 2 represent
the CODONS in the single strand
model of messenger mRNA $\neq$
a thinks he has solved the problem of consciousness. b knows that a has not done so and now tells us so funnily.

a: I have s— I have s- I have s- I have s- I have something seemingly clever to say.
b: [Badly suppressed, indeed barely suppressed, spluttering, hawking, clacking, nose-trick laugher]

Our Ken sleeps as a houseboy.
Ring his bell. 'You are waxwork houseboy' There!
　　　Dead wrong as trees are cemented
so tight the natsh is reduced stain agent.

　　　He was interested in getting through,
he was this blank and dead to the sound
　　　that came from the higher through-ness flap,
and hard by legal loopholes cracked up to be.

　　　Our Ken is one shut out in body
from World Zionist Organisation Settlement
　　　now lying in our BATHOS with his genit-
alia's barbed halo, to scream for thus far.

　　　He pulls away in mind at his
'hopeless, dreary, broken land' homogenised.
　　　He pushes forward in body
as the neat toddler makes a citizen's arrest.

　　　There is a favour-burst as the
pushing continues, for souls are sodium
　　　light mere tackles; nothing in his
garden but the ghost of a tree.

And what's more...

　　　His house is on the south side of
comfort zone. They take the toothless lead
　　　pouring tea on their cornflakes, power
drunk rubes. Lads! Shoot the sky again for me

please. I was innerested in nothing,
my mind the body supervenes on lustily
   null. One could dance through life
alone, but for inhalers and those creams.

   He pulls away in mind like projectile
vomiting thinking again. He pushes forward
   like a white flower somersaulting
downhill in settler shit. Two deep structures
   for Shooting settlers is/are dangerous.

K. MONJOIE: Off to a ball in Oxford, like to a Mr. Hornblower. Paid in full. Good luck to you, Sir.

K. MEDINA: No representations, columns in every scene like to a coloured plate in a vision textbook, haunted by East Asians. We watch as to your cuckoo centred and high as a dream.

K. MONJOIE: I bring good cheer, shandy-wine, and meatables. I bring a general raising of the mean.

K. MEDINA: Why abseil down with these baubles, this towering black wood coffin-cartoon for pre-schoolers?

K. MONJOIE: I press forward in body and you press forward in body; we both pull back in mind. QED. Such as it is.

MR. HAYE PAULA: I suggest you both melt. In bile and coffee-foam encourage the Absolute Shall.

BOTH KENNETHS:
    x / x /
You rise and take
    x / x /
your nightly rest.

MR. HAYE PAULA: I lived in a Kenneth district, with Ken roads, and Kenny coffee outlets. All phone companies were 'K.E.N. speak'. Got the idea? Every tile on my roof—it transpired – had 'Kenneth M.' transferred onto its underside. We worshipped each weekend in a drained pool, pre-schoolers stood around the edge with hoses. We sang "Ode to Ken'. And you are tired of the motif!

K. MONJOIE: I'll draw a bath for you each day, but will not guarantee that I will not spit in it. Recursion!

K. MEDINA: Al Yawm khamr wa ghadan imr [1]

> Listening for the pink petals
> falling down to a blanket while
> writing the latest Baby-stoning-play
> such I fell, as it were, for
> this body till her mind pushed
> forward & the tree ghosts
> danced above the poisoned stump.

---

[123] Today drink the wine; tomorrow is another day' (Arabic motto)

Everything changed today though. The Three Stooges (Modrick, Shine, and me], plus one or two flotsams, were watching evening TV, about two hours ago. I only wanted to see the BBC news at ten, but the other two were glued to a Channel Four documentary on the parents of murdered and abducted children. I should have left of course, but a kind of recklessness came over me. "Can you jump that gap? There's a hundred foot drop if you don't make it. But look, if you take a long enough run it will be a piece of cake." Something builds in you, made up of the desire to have jumped, and thus to have won the euphoria and ego-burnish, together with the stomach-acid-fear of being a coward to yourself. I stayed. What would have been the equivalent here of having jumped successfully? Simply to have seen her and felt nothing, or better, felt the old irritation with her.

They interviewed her at home. Thank God The Toilet was not there too sitting beside her on the sofa patting her hand. She looked dauntingly different. It was only a change of hair and make-up, but, you see, these were the signs of a decision to look that way, which was in turn caused by her being a completely new form of Sabbine. She looked like a cross between the beautifully pale-n-frail Nicola Roberts from Girls Aloud and a whore – maybe a high-class whore, but one of long-serving. She looked a bit spotty – which one normally associates (who is 'one' here, Jackie boy?) with porno actresses and whores. The hair: She used to have, of course, A-for-Andromeda hair, ruler-straight, pure blonde, centre-parting, long. Now it was subtly permed, redish-blonde, and with a fringe that teased her eye-lashes. Make-up: She used to be sparing with it and her lipstick was light pink. Now the lips were red-purple and the eyes had as much kohl and shadow as a Rolling Stone woman circa 1973.

She did not speak like 'my' Sabbine. She was slurrily soft-voiced, more rehearsed than robotic, forthcoming for God's sake; though still as full of cliché and off-target predications as before ("My life was decimated by a man I trusted, by a man I loved"). She was holding one of Nobby's cars like a well-deserved Oscar.

What did I feel, above all? Lust, simply lust, fuelled by a memory with rich phenomenal content.

But that was not what was bad. This was what was bad. Modrick said to Shine…

Wouldn't kick her out of bed, would you, Phil?

I believe there's a theory of emotion (William James?) that says that we don't run away because we are afraid, rather we are afraid because we run away. Act, then feel. Well, I acted first – verbal action of course; what else from me? – and as I acted my anger became like a solid, mind-independent entity you might walk around or touch. What's more, a script had been written for me, one partly of suppositions, which I delivered with a speed and fluency I observed as a homunculus. My voice was loud and high.

JC: "Kick? Kick! Yes, it would be your leg wouldn't it, Facey? So Jenny tells us, your leg is the only part of your body that ever extends straight when you are in bed with her. You limp, gormless, defective creep!'

MF: [looking down at his feet]: "Now that's tidy, innit, Phil?"

JC: Ooo that's TOIDAY, innit, Phil? That is TOIDAY, you long streak of puss. Your wife despises you, your son despises you, Phil Shine despises you, the people who pretend to laugh at your second-hand wise-cracks despise you; and you despise yourself. You look like a shred of sculpted lard and your breath smells of old urine but you can imagine the counterfactual of going to bed with Sabbine Stripentau [yes it did cross my mind that maybe this was not, in fact, a counterfactual but…] You really are an imaginative stream of snot, AIN'T you, Mod?"

MF: "Thank you very much, monsewer."

JC: "She and you. The Goddess and the glob of toe-jam. The Priestess and the dog turd turning yellowy green in the sun. The sad, beautiful woman and this fifty year old abortion."

MF: "Thank you very much, monsewer"

It carried on for a couple more minutes. My insults grew still baser and more formulaic as my voice grew hoarse; and to each one of them he said

Thank you very much, mon sewer [124]

never once looking up.

Another theory is that animals have a mechanism that inhibits further aggression when we see their opponent is too weak to fight back or when he humbles himself by, literally or figuratively, offering up a soft body-part. The press once called me a psycho-

---

[124] Craigie moved from his usual italics into cursive here.

path. I AM one. I saw that Modrick was crying but I just ploughed on. At a pause for breath, Shine said "Shut up, you bastard." Shortly after, I left and came up here, into the warm arms of the Paddy bottle.

18th November, 2007

I did not go into breakfast today. Guess why? Instead I covered the waterfront, or rather patrolled the prom from the pier to the *Salthouse,* turning smartly on my heels to the self-command of *Wheel!* at the end of each march. The building at the entrance to the pier is a once-splendid but now-boarded-up *Royal Pier Hotel*, built from big blocks of dull grey stone – but *castellated*. It lent the homebound leg a kind of poignancy. It was my Secure Base where I was to be protected from my nasty-clown self, honoured in the mead hall with venison roasting on spits, with foaming horns of ale, with minstrels, and not egg-and-cress, a choice of speciality teas, and *The Power of Love*. It was too a childhood castle, really-made from cardboard in Elstree. Alan Ladd (was it?) in *The Black Prince*. The wonderful scene in which he proves the sharpness of his special sword by chopping through a thick piece of armour as if it were a pine log. Or the genteel battlements of a home-counties mansion in a movie starring Margaret Lockwood. Or the dark profile of 'home' in a Daphne du Maurier love-ghost-tangle on a foamy coast with cocktail cigarettes which one assumed to be in pastel shades beyond the black-and-white image. Remember the brand called *Matinee* – plum-coloured flip-top box with cream stripes, if memory serves.

"If memory serves"! You used the phrase un-ironically. Come on, admit. What next? "Another pint of wallop, if you'd be so good, Mavis." "Chop-chop!" "Are you ready for the off?"

Look. Even if you survive this – which, of course, you shall not – you will do so as a kind of Duffy Clayton[125]. Or rather as a cross between him and Duffy Power[126]. "Aaaah Constable Dixon, so nice of you to call round. Slippy Fives? I ain't – I haven't encountered the toe-rag, I mean the fellow, all week. But do please admire my latest acquisition, a compact disc, and do mark that it should be enunciated comPACT, by a wonderful new unison-singing 12-piece called the *Clit-Loads*. In my humble opinion they are the new *Girls Aloud*." The episode ends with a shot of Duffy in his hovel. His head, supported by his chipped sink, is lolling, shut-eyed, in his bomb-site chair while *You Keep a Knockin' (but you can't come in)* bashes on around him.

I didn't get back to Nimrod till after eleven. And I was in time to see Modrick returning from somewhere with a new species of smirk. "Look Mod," I tried, "if you're still talking to me can I just say I'm sick with shame for what happened last night. The fact is, I'd just had some bad news about my daughter and that Sabbine woman sort of reminded me of her. This sounds ridiculous, but *nothing personal mate*. I have been a complete shit". "That's all right, old chap. It's not the first time my banter has got up somebody's nose. I'm content now. [*content!?*]. Anyway,

---

[125] A character in the classic '60s cop show *Dickson of Dock Green* (lampooned in *Private Eye* as *Dicks out in Dock Green*). Duffy, played by Harold Scott, was an upper-class tramp who had been lucky enough to find a room in which to sleep and play his beloved long-playing records of romantic music, especially Beethoven. His reading too was of 'the classics' –Dickens, Tolstoy, etc.

[126] One of Larry Parnes' stable of manufactured rock-and-roll singers from the late '50s/early '60s. He was a curly-haired rough-neck.

I'll be slinging my proverbial hook on Friday, so, uh, good luck with your book of poems. Funny, isn't it? I'm going on 'poets day'[127]. I laughed like a kookaburra and slapped him on the back.

Then I came back up here and happened to look again at number 36. Two words came to mind: Why? and Shame. At the time I was writing it I as in the mood and it felt like I was making a long sequence of aesthetic decisions. But in looking at it now it's in a new frame. Its proper frame. I see the bare workings of a mind choosing between "This'll do"/"This may do better" or "I can get away with this better than this", or "Why not this... oh hell, why not." OK, I might try to hide behind the idea of it's being pastiche or version; but it's too lazy even for that. Do I not know in my heart that as poetry it is a show-off toddler doing his version of ballet as mum and dad watch the real thing on TV. And it has about as much momentum as a clumping, pouting toddler, or indeed a fifth Form *Waste Land* home-work exercise.

Is all this mood-induced, or is it a relaxing into truth like Duffy Clayton into his commode-chair. Dunno mate. Tomorrow is another day.

---

[127] Thus called for the following reason: Piss Off Early Tomorrow's Saturday

22ⁿᵈ November, 2007

I started this period in bed, half-pretending to have "a bug". I feel not so much ill as weak in spirit and consequently exhausted. The invented symptoms are sore throat, aching limbs, blurred vision (razzle-dazzle 'em!); but really I'm sick of being conscious, sick of all I know and desire. I knew it would last about three days – a trend since childhood.

Jason has been bringing me sandwiches and I have been giving him money to fetch me *Paddy*, a couple of Stollens from the German deli, pork pies, the usual *Mars* and *all* the papers. In fact the lad has been great. As Modrick could never be seriously claimed as a father by any rational soul the role seems to have fallen to me. At least I talk to him and in doing so take him seriously. Jenny does too, but from Modrick all he gets is mock gravity and mock-mocking. What's more, he's bought me, via Amazon, a copy of a brand-new collection of pieces on contemporary poetry called *Collaterals*, with a chapter by – yes, really, he is in the building – by Prynne himself. Well, it's a letter.

37: Dead or Alive

Who did kill the wasps saw
them burned to cinders?
How is knowledge of middle-
sized dried good possible with
McTeaby or Teddy Bears still
lingering in the Chianti & the
world all Rainbow Roller pink?

Outside the sense all snugly
cased ambivalent cars are
made solid by a glance you
might see a streaming out
or insect-wing screened a
reddish green or bluish
yellow, misty as a kitten

in a box, waves nudge the
dirty shore cries for company
by the moon-side gaggle
inside the morning school
might propose at least
a ha-ha epiphany on target
to the further shore adrift

for invisibility mere light
rays in cold murk let's shut
our eyes children and think
with one voice of our little
beds – don't tell me you are
alone in the world like a snow
flake your bed is tethered to

your brain and your dreams
to what is the case till some-
thing is decided for us: night
hawk or night fox, bad or
good dream of your dead
twin how happy he or she
is un-tethered from the waves.

I was not up to reading it initially, being more in the mood for the papers and Jenny's *Hellos* and *OKs*. Talking of J. she did bustle in a couple of times. Once she even sat on my bed and gave me her views on Gordon Brown ("a boffin cast adrift" just about covers it). She has, I think, simply given up on me. That's fine. Women have given up on me more times than I've had hot dinners. But what I cannot cope with is her simply losing interest in me as a – I'm sorry my dear but I must say this – as a, as a... as a *man*. That will not be tolerated. Mod has gone now but there is not even a sideways glance at me. Her body is as neat and brisk and even as... I think I'll abandon this sentence. If I could only manoeuvre the phrase '*Lagavulin* night' into the conversation somehow and gauge her reaction. I am, in Mandelson's phrase, 'intensely relaxed' about her jumping on my bones.

At one point she came in looking for the cat, thinking it might have got into my wardrobe. "It's either alive in there or it's not," I said, "like Schroedinger's". She got the reference. "I did do A-level physics you know, Duncan." This lead me to think harder about Jenny, and it gave rise to the little pot-boiler of number 37. (It also lead to some Jenny-directed thought+action, which I shall pass over in silence.)

Eventually, I did pick up *Collaterals* and turned first to the chapter on *Marty*. An interesting piece on the poem as being concerned with narcissistic love. The idea seemed to work, as least for *some* of it. Good. But why not ask young Grantin himself whether the analysis is correct, as he's only 60 pages away? I really wanted something on its quality, or on what *gives* it its quality. I think I'll come back to this later. When I did turn to Storn'way's piece I read the first two pages and found myself shouting in a brassy and maximally camp voice. YOU CAN GO OFF PEOPLE, YEW KNOW!!! Jenny was outside and this made her put her head round the door to see if I was having a fit, seeing monsters in my 'blurred vision'.

I finished the chapter, decided I was better, got up, dressed, left the place, and walked without aim in the windy, freezing, sleety weather. I had recently 'invested in' a big, electric-blue waterproof from a shop with a name like *@Everest* and wrapped in this I relished being out in the world of things and water.

The maybe-disaster of my Medina 'poem' and now the somewhat-tainted plum-cake of Storn'way's essay. They had done me in with the whole business of word-strings on paper. I had to get out to where there were other things to confront – cars, the estuary/sea, pub-signs, a bandstand on a modest promontory. The walk cured me; though I suspect I could also have been cured by reading an eight year old's letter home.

It's not that Storn'way's prose is unintelligent and uninteresting. He is for sure highly intelligent; but so too is George Steiner, so too is Freddie Raphael, and so too was The Reverend Casubon[128]. And he has a marsh-gas charisma; but so too does Nicola Roberts[129]. These things just aren't enough in this context.

Of course, it was worth reading (e.g., informative about Prynne in relation to Charles Olson) but it was – now I could be thick and missing something, but here goes – like a kind of pretend play. It was a demonstration of what a piece of philosophically informed discussion of (mostly early) Prynne might look like, rather than being the thing itself. It was a representation of what academic prose generally looks like without... *Got the idea*! Footnotes could rise half-way up the page like damp, or rather like undergrowth in which figures such Kant and Hume could be quietly duffed up. No... it was almost the opposite: footnotes were the backstage area, but behind a glass wall so the rock star's audience could see just what appetites he really has and what sensualities he is really capable of.

But now Marx. If I know anything I know my Marx; I lived, ate and dreamed Marx for 35 years of my life. And I also know when somebody is dropping a casual aside that is supposed to look like some revelation of the mind-

---

[128] A character in *Middlemarch* by George Elliot. His grand theory was "not likely to bruise itself unawares against discoveries: it floated among flexible conjectures... it was as free from interruption as a plan for threading the stars together."

[129] A member of *Girls Aloud*. She has already been singled out by Craigie. A pale thin Scouser who often looks lost.

boggling scale of his scholarship. An old trick and it usually works. This is not confined to the academic domain. Take Victoria Beckham. When little Posh makes sure she is reported as saying that for her to become Lady B. to his Sir David would be "*camp*" she is pointing to her non-existent hinterland of cynical, edgy, sophistication of which she dreams. [*Och! Faire tae much thought has gone into this, Moira!*] And it's actually more pompous than a Victorian display of fustian learning. As for Marx, so too for Kant, Hume, Heidegger and the others: the thinker is introduced, a deep knowledge of the work is casually intimated, whilst he is backed away from in custardy phrases.

So what's the defining flaw in this kind of stuff? (OK, of which I have read almost none; but nobody's listening so I can say what I like.) It's that the name of the game is interpretation, of the kind that invites improvisation. You take a theme (political radicalism in Prynne) and you take a chord-sequence (a sentence, literally, a single sentence from Marx) and then you dig into it like John Coltrane extracting all the afforded scales and arpeggios; then you do it again for another few words or some notion you have come across, dig in again and move on to the next one. Like Coltrane there is virtuosity aplenty, but also a slightly-sharp intonation and an icily lacerating tone here and there. It is, in short, essay-writing by iterated, modular, improvisation[130]. If you pick up anything of interest about Prynne from this it will be by chance – a collateral gain, ironically enough.

---

[130] Even quite a cursory examination of Storn'way's essay shows that this is a travesty. Craigie was clearly overwrought when writing this. Some of us at Th.R.U.S.H suspect his personal decline was beginning around this point.

Let Storn'way put his interesting mind to this. Why is Prynne good (on his view); not why does he find the kind of this Prynne does sympathetic, but why is it good as art when set against other ways of writing poetry? And what makes a good Prynne poem better than a bad one? Saying it's 'electricity' to Larkin's 'nougat' is not good enough here[131], but what we are doing, not pretending to do but doing, is writing an academic essay.

Oh yes, now ain't I the uptight, upright, miserable git and killjoy odd socks! No, actually, I'm not. [*Och Moira, ah can see yew wish you were back at yoour wee desk in Glasgee.*]

I will tell you why I'm not. It just happens to be the case [*Och, yooo're fair burstin' wi' modesty, Moira!*] that conceptual thought is one thing, a constraining thing, and imaginative writing is another thing, in which you are free at every point. Of course poetry should be intelligent, as it should be "well written" (Auden), but by and large poets are not at their best when doing conceptual thought. Larkin admitted in an interview that he was hardly capable of it. And when Stevens came to write down in prose his essentially poetic ideas about metaphysics in *A Collect of Philosophy* he fell flat.

The question is then [*Oh dooo go ON, Moira?*]: Can formal disciplines such as analytical philosophy and linguis-

---

[131] In a surprising discussion about the merits of J. H. Prynne on Radio 4's *Today* programme around this rime, consequent on Prynnne's being lauded in a recently published overview of modern poetry, Iain Sinclair said that comparing Prynne to Larkin was like comparing electricity to nougat. John Sutherland was the (characteristically ameliorative) co-discussant.

tics, especially the computational kind, illuminate what poets do, and can they serve as any kind of poetic grist. No. I can see a sense in which highly *un*-analytical philosophy – Heidegger's maybe – may spur the philosophical imagination, as it may have done (I learned from *Collaterals*) in the case of W. S. Graham. Oh I really don't know where I'm going now with this P. C. Plod stuff. Here's just one little fact I'm fond of. Gillian[132] told me about a young guy who joined English last year. He started his Ph.D. exploring Stevens' verse via Montague semantics[133]. The project was abandoned. But just imagine the realm of these commonalities. Not commonalities, what can we call them... dunno. Funny old research programme anyway. You throw a plank between the poetry and some computational linguistics while the bits of each on which this plank rests are bound to be the *least interesting*, the boringly solid and un-*sui generis*, in each. But then again, I could well be a philistine. Wouldn't put it past me.

I'm probably wrong about this, but I'm just feeling unpoetic – do I ever actually feel *poetic*? – sceptical, un-or-disillusioned. In fact I'm feeling just like the Glasgow bruiser Craigie, whom some of his idiot colleagues, the ones who roam the swamp-lands of post-structuralism, accuse of being a 'positivist' (which I am not, and which these berks can't even define), of being a 'logic chopper'

---

[132] See footnote 12

[133] Richard Montague (1930-1971), a highly influential logician and philosopher, held that natural languages like English could be precisely formalised using the technical apparatus of logic. His treatment of meaning was distinctive in that it was set out in terms of truth conditions and entailment relations, of the mind-external rather than the mind-internal.

(a term they will have picked up from a Tom Stoppard play), and the possessor of a 'chi-square mentality' (chi square being a simple statistical test they are too innumerate to run).

Merry thoughts of this kind engaged me on my walk. But I felt buoyant, dizzy even. The rain was bucketing down, there was no moon, I was practically the only person about on the prom. But the view from the blown-over-tree promontory was wonderful on both sides: the *Salthouse* to my left gave a bright basic welcome and to my right there was the brittle elegance of the pier and the sweet cod-medieval dream of the old hotel. I was falling in love with Clevedon, for want, of course, of any human alternative. The song *Old Cape Cod* came to my mind. The bandstand was right behind me. I clambered up on to it and decided to perform the song to the estuary, with improvised lyrics. I didn't particularly want to get picked up on suspicion of drunken – I was not – carousing, so I had to do it in a low voice. A Michael Holliday [134] pastiche would be ideal here, so I even stuck out my chin and swayed lugubriously.

> *If you're keen on sand storms that lash the air*
> *Quaint little troglodytes with gritty hair*
> *You're sure to fall in love with*
> *Old Cape Cod.*

---

[134] Michael Holliday (not his real name) was a Liverpudlian merchant seaman who become the British Bing Crosby. He died by his own hand in 1963.

If you like the taste of sea-slug stew
Served by a widow with designs on you
You're sure to fall in love with
Old Cape Cod.

Winding sheets that seem just made for you
Crones whose legs spur thoughts of Danish Blue
You're sure to fall in love with
Old Cape Cod.

If you spend an evening then may I say
Storm clouds shit poison over Cape Cod Bay.
You're sure to fall in love with
Old Cape Cod.

I wondered home (*home!*) with thoughts on the tragic but completely-of-his-time Michael Holliday. When back, I picked up a little book bought from the second-hand section in the pottery by the *Moon and Sixpence,* called *A Day with Byron* by May Clarissa Gillington[135]. This lead to the chopped up prose of number 38, about 'the morning of' a figure in the Holliday mould. I don't know about the gay insinuations re MH though.

---

[135] Folcroft Library Editions, 1977

38: A Day with Jordan

A July afternoon in 1959
Johnnie Jordan rising to the sound of
motor horns and the Light Programme
from a bed 'littered with loutish leavings'
(good friend's phrase).
Sure the mood is low-key
Sombre, almost so.
He puts on clothes & empties ashtrays
& toying first with tea-bags makes
tea & lights some leaves ('Passing Cloud')
he gazes out
over the hot evanescence of South Ken.
Last night perhaps:
The Six-Five Special
then supper with sweet people
on pulsing to *The Strawberry Room*...
Right now
he feels he really does and quoting *The Daily Mirror*
that he's "England's Answer to Guy Mitchell."
He may perchance hear
himself sing radio small:

> *Hey where you goin'?*
> *Hey can I come?*
> *Hey what's the hurry?*
> *Stay have some fun!*

Where do we come from?
Hey do we care!
If only you'll linger in my lagoon
I know we'd have our share
Of fun and... (pause)

Hey where you goin'?
...

A smile creeps across his youthful face
he pushes
back a lock of his
thick thatch, unnaturally black against
his naturally pale skin.
That was his first hit and still
a number most requested giving
pleasure untellable.
He lolls he knows in many a heart.

But hark! His reverie is broken
by the arrival of his mates.
Could be:
Conway (Russ) or Holliday (Mike),
Joy or Babs Beverely.
Often and often wished if not it's his ol' mate
Freddie Mills.
Today Russ and Freddie.
Freddie may hold forth more than likely
Freddy will.
Clapping Johnnie on the back
and with a twinkling eye he tells a tale –

a tale perchance the doings of Digby Wolfe
the contretemps of Terry Dene.
"You kill me, Freddie," Russ murmurs, still
with that Bristolian burr.
"Shoo! you two," says Johnnie his spirits
rising and his steps a-skip
"I'm late, late, late!"

Russ toying with the ivories
of the Jordan upright
Freddie flexes &
Johnnie brushes teeth.
"Blay dat bid again! "
Gurgles through the distant foam...
A rambling line with a hint of backbeat,
a supple, loping melody
that Johnnie can't fight
he leans
like a lizard against the 'ol Joanna
and improvises gives vent - he just
can't help it

> *Oh where where is my heart?*
> *Oh where where is the key?*
> *How oh how did we part?*
> *And how, how could you leave me?*

Then from the kitchen...

> *Is? Is it time for tea?*

"Oh you kill me, Freddie" says Russ.
Johnnie grabs his car-keys and tells them

to let themselves out.
"What's bitten him?" says Russ.

How the fuck, the fuck should I know?

sings Freddie planting a bear punch -
rough and tumble prelude for the chums.

Johnnie's car a little French job –
the skyblue-blue of blackcurrant pastille tin
with similar substantiveness. Lunch (late!)
with his agent Marge. Taskmaster Margarie
Marge the major-domo, Mad Marge of Maida Vale.

The day was red white & blue
a little English
job. The best weather all his friends agreed
they all said the weather was
the most the best day &
last he enjoyed before his first and
last overdose.

24th November, 2007

... And talking of Montague Semantics [*Stop! Where are you going?*], here is a nice, illustrative case. Till now my quaint miseries have been inner, mentally mediated & merely triggered by social events, but from a day or so ago they have suddenly come to have neatly extensional causes, touchable, inert – rich referents in the physical world. The misery's meaning is sufficiently explained, is exhausted by, their worldly cause. Given up yet? OK I really know bugger all about Montague Semantics. Let's just say I'm simply in the shit, shit that requires urgent action by me & not merely social shit: it's money shit and therefore food-and-drink shit, roof-over-the-head shit, standing in the rain with your suitcases shit. This happened yesterday. Let me take a deep breath first.

I had been listening over and over to the Mike Heron[136] song...

> *Deep is the river running through my life*
> *And full shines the sun upon it.*

Listening to this filled me with optimism and gentleness. And then.

Shortly after breakfast I was chatting to Jenny in the dining room, and she was gazing out to the road. I recall the croissant profile (which has humanised now in my mind) against the privets. "Oh fuck!" she said, "Here comes

---

[136] A member of the sixties' hippie folk duo *The Incredible String Band*. This song is from his only solo album *Smiling Men with Bad reputations*. See poem 40.

Crazy Pavey. What the bloody hell does he want?" Two minutes later she came back looking her version of sheepish. "He wants you, Dunc. Good luck."

This was Detective Sergeant Keith Pavey. Pavey of the (Back) Yard. There he was in the hall-way grinning like a delighted schoolboy. I felt merely numb. I did not think "Well, this is it then". This clearly was a silly man who nobody would trust with picking up a murderer. And he was alone.

We went up to my room. He was short with an enormous belly, wearing a cheap blue suit too small for him. He had an impressively think brush of black hair cut short-back-and-sides. His face: one could easily imagine it pushing up through the skin of an apple. It was a face perfectly constructed for jet-stream spitting and calling women 'the bint' or 'it'. The mouth was a wide thin ambiguous flap above which, cut with a craftsmanship of which you wouldn't think him capable, was a perfect pencil-line moustache. The effect he was after was probably Charles Bronson, but this was spoilt by two things. First, he looked like he had forgotten to put his teeth in, or, more likely, his front teeth had worn away. Second, his flesh was a morass of sagging, flimsy strata which looked as if it would flop off at one emphatic nod. But it was impossible to conceive of any emphatic actions being from him. Only his immovable grin was emphatically itself; while the rest was tentative, almost girlish. His eyes sparkled through the Audenesque ruin of his face, like silver dragées in a relaxed meringue.

Got the idea!!!!!

He'd started by saying he had heard I was a poet. I gave him my story while he nodded sagely. "I don't really see the point of poetry," he said, "if you don't mind my speaking my mind, Sir. Okay for eggheads, women and fairies, I suppose."

He spoke further. It turned out that he was a 'mate' of Modrick's. Modrick – certainly, after my outburst a few days back – had gone to see him. In short, Mod had told him I was fishy. Two reasons. I had neither credit card nor cheque book and paid all my bills in cash. (How did Mod know I didn't use a cash machine? No matter, for he was right of course.) Two, while I was "supposed to be" a poet, none of my products were really poems at all. They were just bits of random or jokey *typing*. Even he (Mod) could tell that, and he was no 'literary type'.

If anything, Pavey's grin grew wider when he'd finished speaking. But then have you ever tried grinning and talking at the same time? (*Have you, dearie, have you?*) He gently asked me to explain my penchant for hard cash. For a few milliseconds, I thought of trying to pass myself off as an Arab. Can one be converted to Arabism as to Islam? I explained that I didn't like "flaffing about" with cards "all the time", so I "tended" to withdraw "substantial amounts" of money at cash points. My voice was drying up, and now Pavey's grin was a ghost of itself. "Can I see the card, or cards, please sir?" "Why?" "Never mind 'why' matey [grin gone now], just show me your credit cards. If you have any."

A half a minute later I was "confessing" that I had just been through a "bitter" divorce. The settlement had been "viciously generous" to my ex-wife, who had been "serially unfaithful" with a string of younger men; and I was "damned" if I would give her a penny, so I just "bolted". "Seemed like a good idea at the time," I added.

"And what have you been living on, Sir?"

"Ah... Now there you have me, as Oscar Wilde didn't say". (I was being hysterically reminded of – was it? – a bit of P. G. Woodhouse in which a cod Oscar Wilde says something like "You know, life is just like a bowl of fruit in which all the bananas have been pre-pealed." "*Why* is it?" "Ah! Now there you have me.")

Do you know what's coming next? Do you, dearie? *Do* you?

"Please show me your cards, Sir."

"Look, I'm sorry but I really don't see..."

"Put it this way. If you don't, I'll take you down to the station and DNA-print you"

I showed him the neat bundles of notes in a battered black box that used to contain cutlery (bought after my first wedding). The box lay buried in my shirt drawer. I had around £18,000. He left me with exactly £600 and a memory image of his happy smile.

"Go and get a carrier bag from Jenny. There's a good boy."

He put some pages from my *TLS* over them and then one of my shirts from the drawer.

"Now look here, Poole, if you breathe a word of this to anybody..." [I was now nostalgic for the grin]... "it'll be the saliva swab for you, swiftly followed by a relaxing sodjunn in the prison library. OK?"

"So I'll be shooting off then. Nice to meet you, and I dare say I'll be in touch. Goodbye, Sir."

I walked the tightrope from the desk to the bed and sat looking out over the Bristol Channel. It is possible, you know, to have no thoughts, just percepts. I knew that thoughts would require looking down, and I did not want to sway and fall. You would have thought that the falling had already happened. You would have thought I had found rock bottom. No, the feeling I had was that of high, dangerous serenity, and the need for company high up here.

I went straight to *The Moon and Sixpence* to sit expectantly with a pint of *Guinness* and a *Jameson* (no *Paddy* behind the bar) chaser. Perfect! A tall, slender, black-clad, black-haired, Jewish-looking beauty sat herself down a couple of chairs away from me beneath the menu board. She moved like an eel. In fact –– now let's not piss about -- like a *simpering* eel. White face, kohl-ringed eyes; her little mouth a squashed raspberry. Can this get any better: She took from her bag and began to read a copy of

Markovitz's *Imposture*[137]. Soon, we were chatting about Byron and I was treating her to my thoughts on Byron's low boredom threshold and my thesis that he mainly wrote verse to excite himself. Actually, I didn't believe a word of that, but I was now on my third brace of drinks. She had allowed me to buy her a glass of white. "Why did he marry Isabella then?" she came back, "probably the most boring woman in western Europe." There was an echo of 'Ah, now there you have me', and I was almost returned to the normal politics of the present. But I swerved clear and said "The promise of her bovine buttocks?" You see, I was playing a Dangerous-to-Know. For a moment I felt devastating, and her eyes flashed.

But then a falling away began when she said she was graduate student at Bristol researching feminist readings of this and that. Of course, she was then treated to my thoughts on 'feminism' and whether men can truly be feminists (*Like, who cares!*).

Completely ad hominem and pathetic. I dried up. To be opinionated in my way there has to be an underground river of adrenalin, an excitement at the thought of being listened to. Don't have that now. I went to the bar to buy us some coffees and when I got back she was cuddling up to a wispy blonde with the look of a young Joanie Mitchell. I was then introduced to her "girlfriend" Janice. And soon they too were 'shooting off.'

---

[137] This is Benjamin Markovitz's well-received novel about Dr. John Polidori, who was Byron's physician for a short period. It deals, in part, with the authorship of the first vampire tale – written by Polidori from an idea by Byron, as far as we know.

I was not going to think. I would not let thoughts through. It's healthy to have money worries. These would occupy my mind nicely. Meanwhile, rather than be J.C., I imagined being a man in love with my simpering eel, travelling away from her after an inadequate visit.

39: Strapped for Words

Full in the eye
as a clutch-bag for all the desired
she turned from the bitter wind
and the curtains were stained
with dust of kohl.

She saw I could not but be
the various black horses listed
on the black-board
that bolt over railings
& onto the track. Oh

to peter out in a field
stone-clear
of this blue flame; for
she is a species away
tilting down a profile
strapping on a simile
standing proud – a princess
ready for her princess.

Something is stalling
in the dark behind cloud-
white houses in this midlands
rain, stalled and stabled,
no vibrations to signal
her words, just
scraggy fields relieved
by coffee sips. Ah!
One Message Received

25th November, 2007

I read through number 39 just now. It's utterly bleached and beached, even farther from meaning than the most Prynnish of my Prynnishes. It is a particular kind of bad poem. Bad in a way that none of the other 38 are bad. What makes it so bad is the kind of prim care with which it is written married to a gross, *Star*-reader sexual imagination.

But today, I am on my feet, strangely cool and sociable. At breakfast, I chatted, like a favourite uncle, to a couple from Bath. And when Jenny asked what Pavey had wanted I just said "case of mistaken identity", adding with a wink – yes, a *wink* – "no, actually, he wanted me to read at the policeman's ball."

I returned to my room and prepared for the government of my finances, as well as to write number 40. It was a balancing act (one undertaken on a carpet) between the brute fact of Pavey and the Mike Heron song that I was loving a bit ago[138]. I did not want to lean on another Prynne poem to write it so I chose one of R. F. Langley's called *Brute Conflict*[139] – chosen for the title. Langley is an interesting, careful, difficult-to-categorise poet. Elderly now and, apparently, an old friend of Prynne. He is difficult in the traditional sense of having a determinate meaning implicit in his poems. Well, that's how it seems to me, Lesley.

---

[138] See footnote 128.

[139] This is from his collection *The Face of it,* Carcanet, 2007.

40: Smiling Men with Bad Reputations

That these things were mine.
They could have been
trash parcels that see
enumeration is not the point
the point I've come to now.
The life pendant on count-
ables is a plateau of normal
science, not wishing back
& noticing the starving air.
The taste of whiskey &
caramel wetting rubber
fingers to count on.
The joy of rain-drops &
sherbet lemons & iron filings
& wet peelings, the joy
of foldable ideas and podia
stretching to more mornings
I have abandoned return.
'This note's for you' I
say to Patel of uncountable
wet goods counting on my
naiveté. Oh if only physics
boxed our notes like petals
or like syntax, but we will
meet the level socially
or else macramé-free.
Four or five hundred re-
main in my secret drawer
hatched subtle & moonily
striped. The smiling rozzer
is alight tonight changing

down. 'You stupid bint!'
he lisps to the old dear
crossing, walking to the
convenience store. Cheap
& ever open. Available afford-
able: my empty hands are
remotely happy in their
own life. Let's sing a song to take
the sense away. 1 2 3:
Deep is ...the open drawer's
simple smile. In just 29 hours
all will be meaningful
meantime to lie willing up to
the soul of
a placid long-haired
singing man uncountable.

OK, so I need money, some money to tide me over till I can find some black-economy job. The only people I can reasonably call upon are my children. (No real friend-friends exist, just lots of people who I went out to play with.) The three ex-wives? One would laugh dirtily and then put the phone down. One would phone the coppers immediately. And one would spend two months seeking spiritual guidance on what she should do. The children then. Nathan? I can see him sitting in his buzz-cut, floral shirt, Armani suit and black beetle-crushers telling the anecdote about his 'papa' to his pals. He would help a little, but he would also deliver a lecture, though not of course one about why killing children is indeed a bad thing. In his world, nothing is bad or good, true or false; though it you did call child-killing a bad thing to do then surely "quite a lot of people would line up behind you" – as I once heard him say apropos water's being wet. No, he would tell me that I had no insight into my motives for anything. Had I interrogated my set of 'explicit' reasons why I had killed Nobby? Who was I *really* killing here? My own son? (This he would say like a solicitor.) My own, hopelessly immature self? Then I would angrily point out... actually, no, I would cave in as I always do with him. We would call a truce and he would probably give me a few hundred or so as I reminded him that his suit and retro shoes together would have cost around £2,000. No, not Nathan.

Francine[140]? She would either refuse, pleading poverty (no word about the act itself and why I needed the money), or she would make some sacrifice designed to humble me. OK, she just might give me a small fortune, courtesy of her put-upon banker husband, but the 'sacrifice' would then be taking the kids out of school to pay for it. In the instant of doing this she would then anticipate my thought: "Now don't tell me they should have been state-educated all along. Who are you, of all people, to tell me..." And so forth. No, absolutely not Francine.

Anne[141]. It would have to be Annie, despite her relative poverty. How could she and Francine be sisters? How could she and Francine be the same species? What can I say about Anne? The way she looks says most of it. (You will have spotted my penchant for list-like physical description. The curse of the amateur writer, Tarquin.)

---

[140] Craigie's elder daughter.

[141] Craigie's younger daughter.

Small, dumpy with helmet hair and pillar-box lipstick that belongs to 1962, a perpetually surprised expression, and a dress-sense that says "Ignore me, I know I'm not attractive; I'm just looking forward to old age." She had had the same boyfriend (now husband) since she was sixteen, a God-bothering school teacher. They could not have children, and while she badly wanted them she would never complain about her fate. She was somebody with very few desires whose main goal in life was to do the decent thing. As a child, she would amuse herself for hours with a colouring book or jig-saw, never asking for treats. She did, though, like watching TV and eating, preferably at the same time, and with the cat on her lap. We were and have remained – this is her word from age two – "pals." The only real guilt I have felt since that Saturday morning in Bearsden came from thinking how all this would affect her.

26th November, 2007

I have just written to Anne asking her to come down here with some cash. I know I'm taking a chance, but they are more likely to tap her phone than sift her mail. Are they? What do I know? I *printed* her address on the envelope.

I told her it had been no more than an accident at bathtime. Why did I run away then? Ah, now there you... (not that again). I said that, first, Sabbine would have been ultra-suspicious and kick up a terrible stink, and that, second – actually this is really both first and second – I had been suffering from... wait for it... *depression*. Look, if it can work for Stephen Fry then why should it not work for me too. Indeed, why should it not work for Hitler!

My diet was bad[142] because it was very difficult to obtain good quality vegetarian fare in the Germany of the 1930s; and this increased my cortisol levels, which in turn reduced the density of my seratonin sites. In addition, my penchant for chocolate cake had, by reason of my severe reactive hypoglycaemia, reduced my blood sugar to dangerously low levels. I could not release my tension by means of smoking and drinking; and this also made me a social outcast. At a deeper level, those explosions that buffeted me as I rode my dispatch bicycle here and there in the trench war of '14-'18 caused neurotic difficulties too familiar from the Freudian casebook to itemise. Moreover, the serial political failure that I experienced in my early career produced in me a condition of so-called

---

[142] At this point, Craigie changed from his usual, ultra-angular italic.

'learned helplessness' in which one feels that all action is futile; and consequently I had lost faith in myself as an agent." But surely," you will reply to me, "you were a very successful agent, with your Reichtag-burning, your speech-making-at-mass rallies, your sovereign-country-invading, your minorities-exterminating — stuff of that nature!" To this I merely reply: "Ah, now there you have me..."

Come on, you can do better than that, Adolf!

"Yes, of course. Now let me see, now. The sense of my being a failed agent, and therefore a destined-to-fail agent, encouraged in me a deep and poisonous jealously of all those humans who are successful agents. Jews: prodigiously successful bloody agents. Gypsies, poofs and commies. Look at them! Acting up all over the bloody bloody place and being all autonomous and pre-emptive and that.
And let me tell you with reference to the invading business, that it was not I — Adolf — who personally invaded anywhere. I only had to nod my head when the generals asked if they should get on with it. It takes little to make a nod of the head my friend! Most of the time I would stay home watching Eva bending over."

Be that as it may, 'depression' was what I said to Annie. The rest of the day had been spent writing two frankly Sabbine-missing poems. I just can't bear to say what I need from her right now. She was a wonderful amenity, then she became a burden, bore, irritant. I escaped in no uncertain terms and now I feel I am in love with her. Feel I am, or am? Same thing.

In fact, the first poem (number 41) was an attempted reconstruction of one I wrote after first catching sight of her in 2006 – 'Early Auden'. Her shy (shy in the way that the Undead are shy) appearance at a drinks party for new lecturers was the occasion. I think the first two stanzas were pretty much what I wrote at the time.

The second one, number 42, began as an exercise. I had been reading Charlotte Mew and wanted to have a shot at one in that style. She was a wonderful poet; but I suppose her reputation was half-drowned in the flood of Poundish-modern. There is a mystery at the heart of her work, and yet the surface is as clear as a tear-drop. And the rhyming! She would never, as somebody once said of the great-rhymer Larkin, 'reverse into' the parking-space of a rhyme. And it was more than being 'organic'. They are sweetly surprising and yet as necessary as the next breath. The amateur rhymer is always prey to shutting down the line too early as if the quarry had been found. (And this is what spoils my poem.) It's what tends to doggerel. But with Mew there is none of this There!-I've-made-it stuff.

This is all bollocks, I suppose, but if I was not joking, or opinionating, or writing verse, or drinking then where would I be, eh? I said *'Eh?'*. I like 42, actually. It's a human poem with zero bullshit in it.

42: *Early Auden*

It's early Auden &
the buds are out.
Some minds are maudlin,
some casting clouts.
When it's early Auden a
fawn of the forest looks
shyly out; her

proud head turned away
as if to say:
"I won't do that again.
I won't go back again, will not
sail back on the floating curse; I'll
try to love myself again.
And if the love I find

in early Auden
is a ghost love, not one
sweet and solemn,
is a love with sweetness stolen
then I'll fix the feeble ghost
in my memory book
and learn a harder look.

42: His Mild Returning

Wildly as a wind-tossed tree – I own this thought –
      Flailing or waving from its heart,
   I rip love open with a dart
Plucked from the careless fingers of one who sought
But seeks no more the wash of my cold sea
Of watery words, now ever on the turn;
She could not hear the words as meant to be:
     As all I'd earned
From my dry strivings in the lea
      Of the black-iron bulwark to all I'd spurned.
      My mind is blank from blankness learned.
The days die young. I die
By neat degrees and watch the rainstorms pock and churn
The soft clay of the cliffs where weak winds sigh.
Meantime I feel her memory burn
Inside me and I say 'I must return.'
God, that I could! That I might only rest my mind
    In her soft bed
      And turn with her until we are spun thread
That floats upon the seaside air this Winter's day.
It is deep pink and buds hang from it as a kind
Of frail but potent wish. I watch the light
      Play on the pebbles, morning clear and tarry night;
      They are the children we have washed away.

James Russell

5th December, 2007

Dear Daddy[143],

Don't worry. I will fly down to Bristol on Monday 5th December and take a taxi to Clevedon because I hear it is not very far away and take a taxi back to catch the next flight home to Glasgow. I will come to your Guesthouse at around 12.45 pm and you can take me out to lunch! I assume there is somewhere nice to eat nearby.

I hope you are feeling less unhappy and depressed now, but that bloody (pardon my French) German woman must take some responsibility for what happened, mustn't she?

See you soon and don't worry about anything.

Love from Annie.
xxx

The exclamation mark. I keep returning to it. So I'll be meeting my daughter in about thirty minutes. Good job I had warned her about my fat-baldy look. Have bought a black pin-stripe suit from Marks & Spencers, I suppose to feel more fatherly and seem less of a lost man. The trouble is that it makes me look like a bouncer. In fact a few minutes ago I put on my sunglasses and did a spot of role-playing in front of the wardrobe mirror, feet planted well apart, arms folded high across the chest, saying in an Eastenders voice "No fahckin ID!" I wonder if Jason

---

[143] Craigie had pasted the letter onto the page (blue biro on blue Basildon Bond, a large hand).

heard this before he came in with news of a poetry reading at the Arnolfini[144]. I told him about Anne's visit.

I write these sentences and they die under me like an old donkey. I'm getting sick of writing. There is nothing to communicate, only an impatience for the end of the last act, so we can all get the last bus home.

In fact, in the last few days I have been trying to recapture the old Duncan Poole of the multiple *Mars Bars*, two-meal deals, manic or industrial-scale boozing; but it doesn't work at all. I *forced* myself to listen to my Little Richard CD. Not even *Slippin' an' a Slidin'* did the trick. There is a German word for how I am – *schwer* –which covers difficult, serious, and heavy. What I really need are (a) the company of light, quick people; (b) intellectual difficulty – something to be mulled over and grasped or falling just out of reach, something to give me self-forgetting in the abstract challenge, not philosophy, not something I can take a view on, but a bit of *refractory* science, impersonal and... oh the donkey has just died; no, wait a minute (c) sex.

I have been trying to educate myself away from my need for Sabbine by imagining her with The Toilet. Now *that* is some kind of fun project. What I really want to do is to go back with Anne, to live in her spare room and be brought cups of tea, reading history and Shakespeare during the day and watching Coronation Street with her and Henry in the evenings. I think of the neatness of their house in Pollockshields, the flowery smell and *The Archers* coming

---

[144] An art gallery on the Bristol docks

on, the Sunday morning routine when Henry makes some 'real' coffee and fries up a complicated breakfast.

6th December, 2007

"You look very... *healthy*, Daddy." Those were her first words. She was dressed as if she had an appointment with her bank manager, and I was dressed just like one. She stood in the hallway beside Jenny, about the same height as her, but Jenny could have been her lunch. I almost said that now we really do look like father and daughter. *Almost* said.

As we walked to the Italian place just along from the *Moon and Sixpence* she would not allow a second to pass in silence, giving me every detail of the journey, including her deliberations on how much to tip the cab driver, and the various pros and cons of booking the same driver back, and exactly how she had calculated 15.45 as the time he should collect her from the *Nimrod*. But what would we find to talk about for all these hours? I felt uncommunicative, but then I did have to act depressed, didn't I? I could hardly be full of silly fantasies.

In the restaurant she rejected my suggestion of having starters as being "too extravagant" and insisted on only having a glass each because of the "ridiculous mark-up" on bottles; and then gave me an A4 envelope containing £15,000 and a new *Waitrose* carrier bag.

"This will keep you going."

"Until when?"

She seemed to draw her first proper breath since her arrival.

"Sorry, I mean. I don't know what to say."

"A nice thank-you would do." She smiled.

"How can you afford all this? Thank you, thank you, sweetheart"

"We cashed in all our ISAs"

Yes "we". She had shared all this with Henry, who insisted that, as a Christian, he was duty bound to help his fellow man, sinner that he almost certainly was in this case.

After this we were awkward with each other. She talked about office politics at *John Lewis* and her new boss and her bigger-this-year bonus. Then in answer to her question about what I did all day I told her I was writing a novel, but had nothing to say about its topic. I stuttered something along the lines of a *roman a clef* about the intellectual corruption of the modern university system. She started to giggle and kept on giggling.

"Oh, that'll be a best-seller then. I can see them stacked up in *Borders*. What are you going to call it?"

"My working title is *You are all Bastards and I Hate You So Much I Could Spit*."

"Do you remember that book you used to read to me called *What Do Daddies Do All Day*? There are plumber Daddies, teacher Daddies..."

"Bouncer Daddies, Deconstructionist Daddes... *sperm-donor* Daddies..."

I caught sight of us in the mirror – two happy babies laughing at this. Shortly after she put on a mock-serious expression and declared that it made better economic sense to buy a bottle than drink by the glass; and so I ordered a bottle of Chablis.

She ate as heartily as ever, but now there was no small talk. In fact, we talked remorselessly about the person who had the smallest small-talk in the world –– Sabbine. Sabbine had always seen Anne as a competitor, and looked petrified in her presence. When anxious she would deal out a kind of passive aggression, answering "Vot to you mean!" to polite enquiries and showing zero curiosity about the what the other person was saying, maybe taking a sudden interest in a loose thread on her blouse. Anne detested Sabbine, and could do a decent impression of her. Henry might ask if she had been out to buy some bread that morning and she would reply 'Vot means you by ziss?"

There was something dangerous, however, in our talk about Nobby. We talked back to when I had taken Sabbine to Sunday lunch with Anne-and-Henry and we had, for some complicated reason, to take Nobby along with us. First, he would not get out of the car, doing his stick-body act. And in the house he was a little vandal, so the visit was torture to somebody as house-proud as Anne. He swung from the curtains and spilt all that was spillable, spat out all that was spittable. He screamed *Scheisser!* at the sleeping cat and called Anne 'Fatty Bum-Bum'.

Anne did not – thank God – ask for details about the "accident at bath time", for the simple reason, it seems to me, that she knew there was no accident. It was our understanding. But the understanding seemed to encourage something darker: a certain satisfaction with how things had turned out, that justice had been done somehow or other. No, not a strong as that. More that we were pushing away the event to a small place.

The sugar-rush of our tiramisus brought more good humour, and I treated her to my impersonation of Billy Bragg, but a *Tory* Billy Bragg still singing, as ever, like a look-at-me-mum 9 year old.

> *I was a lawyah*
> *I was a bankah*
> *I was a biz-niz-main*
> *Between the wars.*

"Don't ever let Henry hear you do that, Dad!"

Henry is a Bragg-man. But the point was to float the thought that I would see her and her husband again in laughter-affording times.

There was just time for a walk along the pier, in the freezing, screeching wind. The cab was waiting when we got back. I went into my Billy Bragg as we walked up Copse Road. But when she kissed me goodbye saying "I don't care what you did. *I'll* always love you, Daddy" the air seemed to leave the world.

43: Walkers' Britain

Annie: the well is lost or bricked up,
the heads we bear are not ours
at all, as the punitive assonant judgement
passes down in buckets' sensorimotor remembrance.
While the day slows down with torsion,
a film of dry ejaculate lifts in light
air & evening cars drive back to basics.
The path is all the journey, for (to be quite blunt)
it rips, with its dog-leg of bramble tonsures,
the poor cloth hanging drear, indeed quite urban
its mud a rare relish: we lose, in last
light, the happy circle. Mourning grows
in our eyes. Our distance was stark
      from that point, circled under
sight-smudging thought, burgeon our past.
The North wind on the pier made us
two small conjoined fists, air niggled quite
weak in the gun-grey water;

                      our walk was envisioned
as a time-out fissure, an eye-drop or bunglette
that, given out of homeliness, postpones
the little tear within the central thought.
                              I love
how the houses are hutch-like and pocked
with mulch-soft or fork-sharp mouldings
of air so urgent to be off.
Windows tell about the curve of hills,
Welsh factories string the vague line as grey dados;
the pier-planks' melting was not noted by us.
        About the melted wood

James Russell

       as brute of hope, the air
       broken like a toddler's drum
in brocaded rhythms, wrought on
grainy droplets: sugar-dust on steel.

7th December, 2007

I tried to clear my head and, to some extent, listening to Poulenc and Charles Ives helped. Not clear the head *of*, but make the mind and memory clear-sighted. I wrote number 43 – another borrowed surface from, again, *The Oval Window*.

It's time to set it all down, and I'll do this in a single sitting. It's now 6 am. I'll pause along the way to do a couple of poems, that *may* have some kind of relevance. I'll not think too much about them.

Here goes. At the drinks party where we met, I kept a low profile – as far as one can wearing a plum-coloured suit with yellow chalk-stripes. "Hello, I'm Jack Craigie". A cool look from under the brow. "You mean chew are Flesh Harry." I thought I had better clear up any misunderstanding. "Yup [this in an American accent, quoting *The Range Rider*[145], God knows why] folks call me Fl*aa*sh Harry." She looked puzzled. "...In case you thought I was *Fleisch* Harry." "I hope *not*." Everything I said she played with a straight bat; but she did not move away. She told me she had come over from Bremen with her second husband Christoph, from whom she was now "bifurcated".

In lieu of punching the air I filled both our glasses.

The party began to break up and I asked her if she would like to come for a bite. We went to *The Ubiquitous Chip* and sat next to some American wine buffs swilling reds

---

[145] A cowboy series on late 1950s children's TV.

around their enormous glasses. Their look-at-me booming often drowned her quiet voice. I told her about seeing Mick Jagger in there (a toy figure in a business suit, with body guards). Now it was becoming possible to make her laugh, as I pretended to spot rock stars: "Look, is that not Reg Presley [in the heat, I forgot she was a German twenty years my junior] sharing a joke over oysters with Buddy Holly?" Then she came out with the only truly surprising thing I had ever heard from her. "I LOVE *The Trogs*, don't you?"

Later, we walked to her car parked off Byers Road. There was a mutual linger in the cheek-kisses, and so I said "Shall we try a proper kiss?" A slight serious nod. I am tempted to parody now Martin Amis on the 9/11 planes: 'A future flash of tongue probe': that kind of thing. Do it yourself. My first thought on 11/9/01 had been "We'll never hear the last of this." And that was how I felt now. This was the confining moment.

We were careful with each other at first. Certainly, she was sexually shy the first few times; though that was in relation to me. She watched me all the time, watched me like the hawk's prey. Not beautiful exactly, being too thin and slight stooped and lop-sided, with a long-stride, unfeminine marching walk; but a Symbolist heroine – secretly wounded, devotional, and only half-real.

44: The Dogs of Love

1

With the legs you turn, patterned in brine.
Cancerous what-ifs pushed deep down,
simply giving in taste and stoke
you lie fast, lidded in pungent force.

2

With looks we move to the next.
Our appetite is teased up, one
entity, tangled in hair sheen.
This feels like a dancing war.

3

From the top we slide down.
Pork melt in puckered point,
loosening a cry. Love forged
in the heat, cutting the heart free?

4

All done in force, circling an end:
the speech to come, shades to eyes
preening in the desert sun.
This war is the light of our lives.

5

Thus the vanquished lie on the field.
Invaded you win, failed
freedom is a good. Such
speech fails the matter – we all know.

6

Kill such conceits with your hands. At
sand circle, the photo-call bares teeth.
It was warm there, passionate
gold long gone. We are lost – amiss.

Then everything changed one day when we were in bed. She had a period so we were only caressing and chatting. She said something touching in her funny accent and I kissed the tip of her nose saying lightly "Love you". "I will luff you FOR EVER. I will neffer neffer leave you. You are my STAR." She still watched me after that day, but this time it was with a look of something like satisfaction. Also, she quietly and carefully told me: "In bed, we will do anything at all you like. Anysink at all. I will enjoy it if you are enjoying it. I luff you always." She was a good as her word. [# 44 – silly attempt to be Iraq-ish about sex, built on *Royal Fern*[146] that turns back to deny itself.]

I recall, as a child of about eight, bursting into tears at the tea-table because I had eaten all my chips first and did

---

[146] A fairly early poem by J. H. Prynne

not have room for both of the two fat sausages. *Mutatis mutandis* Lonnie, and you have the situation as then. My only concern was appetite management and contention-scheduling. But a heavenly kind of problem.

And now for the worm in the bud. Before we met, she had been scanning (her word) web dating-sites for men. She "interviewed" scores of them, and had rejected many without meeting up. But, as far as she could, she kept in touch with all the ones who were "nice guys" and not "from working class." These were her "friends", to whom she "chatted" (emailed) endlessly. If we had a dispute about something or if she wanted advice I could not give, she asked "my friends" or "my Dumbarton friends" or "my engineer friends" or "my friends who know of kitchen things." She spoke of them as does a Spiritualist of those who had gone beyond. In her Symbolist world they had – no, that's just silly.

For her, 'friend' meant somebody who would respond when she typed.

She had had, though, one web-met lover, and this was Dr. Barry Ritter, a media-friendly, COE of a big teaching hospital – a.k.a. The Toilet; as my never-to-be readers will recall.

I asked her why it hadn't lasted. He seemed like a catch after all, his photograph often appearing in the local press, looking like a cross between Gordon Brown and a night-club proprietor, sleek but with a grin that suggested a smear of ordure above his upper lip. "I thought he was play-man. I did not want to be just only a nowch on his bedstide."

She *still* met him "for coffee". "Why?" "What for 'why'?" His is my friend only now. He is a nice guy only. He is still in luff with his dead wife and his mother is dying in Yorkshire. Leaf him alone, with your Kerry Glitter!" Then the truth emerged.

It had all been going quite well with The Toilet (except that he had "an acorn-type penis") until he began to suggest that "as he could not be enough for me" (the acorn?) that it would be "a good event" if "about four or fife young men" went to bed with her alongside him, and that "in a perfect vorld" these men should be under-age. She baulked at this, and things finally got too much when he begged her to let him video her seducing a fifteen year old friend of his son.

But this was not the worm. This was the worm. When I banned her from seeing him after hearing this, she would get angry in her own special way: sour-faced and mumbling in German to herself, answering my words with weighted pauses or evasive questions, saying that she was "fucked off" that, say, I did not eat all the dull pasta she had cooked and "fucked off" that there was no child-seat in my car. And the plaint, the constant plaint... "You stop me from meeting with my FRIENDS all the time!"

"You can see any of the other losers but not the bloody Toilet. And if you don't understand why, then you will never understand my explanation."

Then I stopped mentioning it; though I'm pretty sure she never stopped seeing him. In any event, she worshipped me, so I just... Well, I just lapped it up.

What to say? What? Don't change the subject. It was clear that neither The Toilet, nor I, nor anybody could really touch her. She needed sex all right, and in a purely animal way she enjoyed it; but there was no intimacy beyond the stuff that a well-placed camcorder could reveal. You could not reach her. What she really enjoyed was the power of dispensing pleasure. And there was something she needed that was far removed from the sexual, something domestic, the warmth of an unobtainable home [# 45]. There was some continuing trouble with her folks. No trauma as far as I could see. They just treated her if she did not count. In fact she would email photos of herself with the kids and they would edit her out after posting the pictures on.

Which drags me to the gristle and lymph glands of the matter: to Ernie, Poe, and Knob-head. That is to say to Erna (thirteen), Paula (ten), and Norbert or Nobby (four). Sabbine's children. To explain the names. Ernie was a big, beefy creature with thighs that rubbed together, taller already than Sabbine. Her hair too was big and coarse, very long and red, and as thick as moquette. If it had been cut short she would have been the ideal extra for *Prisoner Cell Block H*. Poe[147] was small and dank and money-loving. 'Poe' because in one of her school photographs she was wearing a white collar over a dark jumper, with her

---

[147] Craigie means Edgar Allen Poe, and is referring to the daguerreotypes taken of him.

black hair in a short fringe, swept to one side and flying away over the ears; she was leaning far back in the chair as if before great heat, her jaw was subtly to one side, and there was a small shadow cast under her nose that could so easily have been a moustache. Her expression was one of patient but ravening discontent. In truth, she was probably planning how to sell copies of the photograph to family members.

45: Sabbine

The driving gloves were perhaps the most interesting part
of our otherwise lacklustre collection.
Our driving voice propelled the lacklustre party
to an early end as
driving loins flagrantly
had done some times in one pm
that something with Sabbine, our love-hen
our rag Daisy.

I, a fashion chemist, saw her eyes
as the carboys of an old-style apothecary
her essences as liquid prisoners gaudy
within their walls of glass.
Here look: purple, gum-green, electric soup
yellow according to her passive emotions.
        "I am a chemist with an eye
        for bare hands. I'll drive you
        home."

              *

But none of the other desperate comedians

none of the public, none of the whole
gin-drinking public,
saw the essence of Sabbine –
that ravening construct.
We never paddled up to it.
It did not lie upstream from her irises
as a swaying hinterland patrolled
by rangers in costumes.
It was systematic, open sometimes to strangers,
lapsing now to a diorama of a winter
evening, which did not show toast
made on an open fire spread with beef
dripping, served with strong tea
in sight of old metals mat
with closure.
It showed the silence of a 6pm
commuter carriage,
the visual field stale as old water
a hunger in the air never to be fed
a longing to be left alone
a longing to be travelling somewhere
other than home.

I had called Norbert 'Knob-head' one day in frustration. Sabbine picked it up and used it herself for weeks before Ernie told her what it meant. She merely called me 'jokerman' and changed it to Nobby. He was disorganised in everything he did, walked like a puppet, and lived for his enormous collection of toy cars. Thin and flimsy [*Och! yooure faire tae keen o' the blinking adjectives, Moira!*] he could behave imperiously: sitting at the table, smiling coldly at his mother, he might suddenly screech in a milk-curdling voice "Apple juice. I Vant it." But he was in a hopeless position, poor little sod, between those two females and this one female. He could be sweetly vulnerable, loved seeing me; and I grew quite fond of him.

She was their mother by biological fact, but her role in their life was that of an ineffectual, self-absorbed older sister. The girls ignored her except when demanding goods-and-services, her son rebelled if she thwarted him, and they all manipulated her, for which she provided the material: their training in the sentence 'I love you, Mummy'. *As I said before for gawd's sake.* Ernie would treat Sabbine like shit, slam the front door so hard a glass panel would crack; but if she prefaced her later text message with 'I love you, Mummy' Sabbine would drive all the way across Glasgow to pick her up from the party waiting patiently in the car as she gossiped her long goodbyes. Poe would say "I love you, Mummy... Can I have a *Twix* bar?" "OK, sweethood." "Can I have two then?" She would give her three [Poe would sell one on], casting a look at me that said "Kids, eh? Can't live with 'em; can't live without 'em." Nobby said it to *everyone*, but knew perfectly well that any kind of viciousness (say, with cat or rabbit or with a snoozing Poe), domestic destruction, or screeching refusal would be forgiven by "I love you, Mum-Mum."

'I love you' was the element we all lived in, so to that extend at least Sabbine could indeed impose herself. Her first words on waking were "Do you still luff me? Did you already go off me in the night?" And if a couple of hours passed without my saying it she would become moody and short with me. I was dutiful in these repetitions, only occasionally doing it in a Bluebottle or Eccles voice[148]. I was bound up in this cat's cradle.

Now, I am not big on planning and thinking-through when it comes to relationships, but this I did know: If I left her I would feel such guilt and would miss her so sorely the sponge-cake world of utterly compliant sex and Craigie-worship that I would soon go back. Then I would leave again, and go back again; and keep on doing this till I would become weirdly dependent upon her and nostalgic for the white lies and routines of 'now'. This has happened before in my little life. But one thing I also knew but did *not* allow properly through: that the only way to really get free would be for me to do something absolutely bad, establish some end-point of no return.

Then the end did indeed come. As I write these words I catch sight of myself in the dressing-table mirror wrapped in this desperate scribble. Oh to be the nonexistent Craigie. Took a short break and wrote number 46.

---

[148] These are characters from the famous radio comedy of the 1950s called *The Goon Show*.

James Russell

46: Sinnlichkeit

There – a kind of Canada
in the glass box, incongruent
with here, identically

different, framed
as a spatial thought, it stirs
a desire: to go through

motions only in a windless
tenement, to be for perfect
moments the hollow twin.

There's water in the drawing
of a steaming cauldron? Sense
between that scalp and chin?

That Saturday morning and I should have been content, happy even. Sabbine had taken the girls to Christoph's, there was the *Guardian* to read in bed (costing me £3.00 to Poe), two croissants and a coffee on the bedside table, looking out onto her garden trees in the gorgeous sun. But my mind was full of scorpions[149]. Or rather they were biting down on me and my babyish, quick-fix habits: reading Simon Hoggard's account of "delicious" meals and "delicious" wines and bad *Virgin* train journeys (oh so different from the round-robin letter-writers he makes money from, ain't it?). I read Marina Hyde mainly because I fancied her; and if she'd looked like Mavis Tumpshie I wouldn't have bothered. I tore out recipes never to be cooked. And the gustatory background to this: the coffee was instant and pissy, as Sabbine never used the *powerful* [thinking back here[150]] machine I had bought her. She had warmed up the croissants in the microwave and not in the oven – she had lied about this – so they were flaccid and friable. She would be back in an hour after food shopping, and we would then spend the rest of the morning trying to have sex between Nobby bursting in knowingly; and would probably end up in the bathroom with the little sod banging on the door. I would then be obliged to stay for a lunch of pizza and oven-ready chips, sitting across the table from Nobby's mechanical rioting. And yes I had no duties, but neither had I projects, and no book to write or even to review. Research had given me up, as had serious thought. Think of my title 'Profes-

---

[149] Macbeth.

[150] See page 2 of the diary

sor Craigie' – like some harmless buffoon from children's television in the Mr Pastry [151]mould.

And where could I go? Because Sabbine would insist on coming with me to see people, after which she should sit in aggressive silence. [*Och, Moira, but what about the lovely sun and the sunny trees!* Piss off you old bat.]

Outside the bedroom I could hear the honking and US-robot voices of the boy's electric cars. Against this I donned the *Walkman* and put in my favourite Little Richard CD. Actually, it does replay close listening – the gusty sax-player who has learned from Lester Young (especially on *She's Got It*) and Richard at once hilariously camp and heartfelt, so much so you wanted, in the words of 2-year-old Annie, to "cuddle him up." A little later, though. I had a mirror moment coming back to bed after a pee.

This was what Jack Craigie had become. It was his *soul*. My distinctive hair looked like a failed attempt at the exuberances that Pinker and Rattle[152] sport, but too long, too straight and too white. [*Och. why always three adjectives, Moira! Have yew yoursel' "learned from" wee Neil Kinnock*[153]*?*] It was a hopeful mess. And beneath it was a silly, half-hearted [*Och, come on one more heave,*

---

[151] A slapstick character from children's TV in the late 1950s, played by Richard Hearn.

[152] Steven Pinker, distinguished cognitive psychologist, and Simon Rattle, conductor of the Berlin Philharmonic.

[153] One time leader of the Labour Party, known to some as 'the Welsh windbag'.

Moira!] goatee. And beneath that the slight white body of an inmate. But far worse than this was the look I shot at my reflection. It was not only that I had (in the words of a neighbour of William Burrough's parents about the young Bill) 'the eyes of a sheep-killing dog' – I loved this phrase and used to waltz Meg[154] round the kitchen singing

> *Your eyes are the eyes*
> *Of a sheep-killing dog*[155]:

these were the eyes and this was the demeanour of my father. These were the spiteful, thwarted eyes of a *little* man. They were eyes that said: "Somebody is going to have to pay for my disappointment and for having me end up so small and so here."

I turned up *Good Golly Miss Molly* very loud, and I was gripping and ungripping the edge of the duvet to it. Predictably, in came Nobby, deliberately pushing open the door so wide it banged against the chest of drawers. He was holding a rally car with yellow spoilers. "Is this a RACING car or a REGLIAR car, Jeckie?" "It's a snow plough. Now bugger off." "It's not a SNOW plough silly face!" Eventually he went away when I told him he could be a big boy and run my bath for me. His tongue tip protruded like a kitten's in concentration as I explained how to put in the plug and turn both taps on as far as they would go.

---

[154] See poem 6 for a recycling of this phrase. Meg is Craigie's first wife.

[155] Presumably to the tune of *The Eyes of A Woman in Love*, from the musical *Guys and Dolls*.

A little later I was listening to *Heebie Jeebies* as he came in again with his sly smile. He was mouthing something, while I was hearing:

> *I'll ring your door till I break your bell*
> *Gonna jump back jump back Heebie Jeebies*
> *Gonna get back get back Heebie Jeebies*
> *Gonna jump back jump back Heebie Jeebies*
> *Gonna get back get back Heebie Jeebies*

He mimed taking off the head-set. I did so. (He could have heard the 'phone, I reasoned.)

"I luff you, Jeckie... I LUFF you, Jeckie."

Es war getan fast eh gedacht[156]. (I recall my translation of this line as a school-boy: 'Premeditation did not blur my mood'. I had been so proud of that.) I starting singing... Come on, Nobby, join in.

> *Gonna get back get back*

etc.

I whisked him off his feet, and was throwing him in the air to the rhythm. He was beside himself with hilarity. This was the Craigie that gave him a break from Sabbine. We moved still singing to the gushing water; and this could so easily have been a TV ad for bath salts in the

---

[156] The second line of Goethe's early lyric *Willkommen und Abschied*: (literally)"It was done almost before it was ever thought."

1970s and not an object lesson in how kin selection operates in humans too[157].

A very little later I was poised like a sprinter on the starting blocks gazing, in what would have looked like philosophic calm, at the pale pink tiles, as beneath me, my left hand on his neck and my right on his lower back, Nobby with surprising reluctance drowned.

When he was finally still and I had lifted him out there was a lot of snot – a glycerine mask of the stuff.

Now here was a something. I thought for a moment he was still alive. Here was his sly grin back. Playing dead? Really, I was *relieved*. How to put this? I felt like a warm human soul in the instant.

Then there was a big posthumous watery belch; after which I wiped his face and tucked him into his bed with his toy dogs and dog puppets. He was still wearing his dog slippers in fact.

I had once asked him which he liked more, dogs or cars. He thought very hard. "I DON'T know, Jeckie. What is the right answer?"

---

[157] This is the theory that animals only act altruistically towards conspecifics with whom they share genes.

James Russell

47: Eight Poems To Live By

1

Only connect
as in
*I am supremely happy
to be thought
a stinking adult*

2

You reach the dock
as the ferry leaves so place
a merry note upon the air
pull tongues
at the sea

3

Be autobiographical as
in seeing the editor
of *The Erotic Review*
at the M&S checkout
& 'twas as if
as some articles
are written before they
are written she
was seen
before… you follow me?

4

As I was dancing o'er the lea
I met a man who looked like me
I was shy but he was charmed
he had two, I had one arm

5.

Paucity paucity paucity
Bakersfield, to be in love/
oh not to be in love
with Alison Goldfrapp
love Belgium instead a
country and as such no
owner of thighs

6

You and your driving
music mother said
light from the kitchen
steady as a bush
against a wall

7

The next one is called:
Tower of Silence -
I ate an orange
over my face was fire focal
sticky for the vultures to come
you think of the first

cut of the grass in April &
the cool cries &
shivering roots
face dried in time due
as the famous primal swamp
in Egypt

8

Marvin my boy
you hard beside the window pane
you turn your face
from ball games
no shatter no
blood & shard none
of that malarkey
only
the glycerine
kiss of death

25th December, 2007

How did it go now?
> *They fold, they pleat*
>
> *They fold, the folding women*
>
> *What is the cleanest thing*
> *in the whole world?*
> *The inside of an unused envelope*

Sitting snug in Jenny's flat with a brandy, as she is supervising supper two floors below and Jason is out with his mates. A vague memory of this poem called *The Folding Women*, by a pretty, dark-haired poet, one of the late-60s London gang. Libby Houston? I'll ask Jason to look her up.

Well, let me tell you that there is one thing cleaner than that, which is the inside of a cigar tube. I puff away. I'm happy. Happy, yes, almost.

This is what happened in the past 20 or so days. After writing down the end of Nobby I found myself living, outward and inward, as a kind of zombie. Actually, I did write a couple of poems, but they required no reflection on my life as now, while diary entries did. Number 49 was based on an unintentionally hilarious puff that Storn'way did for a Cambridge poet's reading, while number 49 was no more than an exercise succubus-ed from a Cambridge lad who is *not* Prynne.

48: Grantin Exemption

Think this think: a poem
uniquely accomplishing a thought

strenuous no not so as petrel-
blue manual on commitment uniquely

imagined surely & truly
think this a song a song

of syllogisms and epistemics:
unique it is in it its mind-buggering

mild-furnishing immensity plucks
it does a living need from the maw

of uniqueness, a unique quiddity
not shaded with smidgens of

Universal no petrel no buy pastel
from the pastel reserves of Universal

no not as to the hearing-aid battery
"swallowable and bright" but truly

universal concepthood containment,
verse project here at home in the

world in habits it has a yes a heaven
heaven surely and solely lured

in lines that once released from the
pen type tokens.

49: Trade Winds

All the true sailing I proposed
our neat circuits of the ocean
fell though that map of brilliant pink
we entranced sometimes

Sea miles that lay distinct from us
with fish with cephalons
jumping out from froth of bulk
these we did not concern

The force of maritime taught us
those small tricks from this to that
with fervent Halloos from my sapient head
the half-on-half censer swung the tune

of the night the day taught
which crowned us clever and lassoed
health from death with strings of measuring
roiled in commonplace

Cruising then at full thrust
from contortion that entrains all air
cutting through with torque to the
slight burr in the mothering wind

Bothered to hide from
not peal the greenly-brown from stems
now that was euphoria!
flapping with sheets of cortex

James Russell

You sang me up by flowing waves
diminish this I won't:
while I loved then lapsed &
steered for shore betimes

Who could dance in the conditions?
maybe those with eyes stuffed by labels
angel-meisters on clouds faded and golden
and worshipped by harpoon gangs

We sketched out the course
was wrenched from meaning
from sighing and vying
from spouting and whalespeak

Finally lost in semaphore
'we are bound homeward'
our nice wee hands on our cloth
lodged tight blood-tight with usage

I did not come down for meals. I was hardly seen and never spoke unless I could not help it. I made no eye-contact. I went for long walks coming home in the early hours stone sober. One evening Jenny asked me if I was all right. Was there something wrong? I stared at her as if I'd been addressed in Swahili and said "lovely job" in a scraping voice.

She followed me up to my room and insisted on being told "What is going *on*?" I again described my situation as 'lovely' adding "working very hard though, Jen." (I had never called her 'Jen' before.) After a few minutes of gentle but futile questioning she said "Come on, matey. Who are you really?" Again (*es war*...) I simply acted, and told her who I was and all about Nobby. In my version though it was more like manslaughter (we had been "playing submarines"). I had panicked thinking that Sabbine ("famously litigious and vindictive") would seek the murder charge.

She saw tears starting in my eyes, and immediately took the tears and me into her bed. It feels like I have been there ever since. I don't know how Jenny manages to be the toughie she is. Being married to Modrick for eighteen years? Buggered-up child-murderers must be a doddle after him. Mod, by the way, has been given his slinking orders, about which Jason declares himself 'sanguine'.

But one lie I did preserve intact in its little glass case was the one about my being a poet. I invented quite an impressive career in chapbooks, prize-winnings, and readings, and elaborated on the visit I made to the Faber offices when they suggested I that "try a sequence in my usual eclectic vein" on which "we would cast a favourable eye, given your track record." This means, of course, that I'll need to go on producing. I think I'll call a halt at around fifty though. Sick of it, quite frankly.

"I've been reading some of them", she said. "They're either... *bohemian*, or just daft, daft as you Professor Craigie. I like Seamus Heaney myself." "Too dutiful for me. I like to mix things up." *Ha!!!*

She looked at the Craigie web-page. "Pity you can't grow it all back," she said.

Today we three ate a goose, and half an hour ago we all sat down to watch *Harry Hill's TV Burp*[158] at Jenny's suggestion. (She said to Jason as HH appeared: "He's using Jack's[159] hairdresser." Watching this show was the first time I've really laughed – I mean not at my own fantasies, not cynically, and *with others* – for about 6 months. Happy? Yes, I sure was then. Let's just see how things go. In some ways Jenny is perfect for me. And no, you old bat, I will not give her a triad of adjectives.

---

[158] A comedy show based around clips from the week's television.

[159] This would suggest that Jason knew now who Craigie was. (By the way, Hill has a shaven head like Graigie's.) This seems implausible. It is likely to have been a mistake by Craigie, so Jenny would have referred to him as 'Dunc' in Jason's hearing.

26th December, 2007

Jenny and Jason are driving up to Bolton today to stay with her mum and dad for a few days, leaving a harassed Maureen in charge. Jenny's parting words to me were "They'll be so chuffed I've got rid of that tosser Mod at last." I saw Jason wince at this. Hardly surprising that he's a deal less pally with me now.

I potter about the flat like the 61-year-old I actually am, making a breakfast of scrambled eggs and smoked bacon, listening to Radio 4, and reading *Private Eye,* something I read from nostalgia only; though one does encounter the odd gem from Craig Brown[160]. Last year I recall a diadem: Christmas carols re-written by Harold Pinter, the agit-prop, grape-shot poet Pinter. I can't recall any of them, worst luck, but something like:

> *Silent night, holy night*
> *All is calm, all is bright*
> *Bush and Blair are showering Iraqis*
> *with shit and blood*
> *stuffing bombs up their arses*
> *saying 'Like that, chummy?'*

It's a mystery how Pinter ever came to write these things. And so *short* some of them; and so keen he was for a good opinion of them. There's a story about somebody being phoned up by Pinter to ask what he thought of the latest

---

[160] A satirical columnist and comic author who has written for a number of newspapers.

two-line wonder about bombs and flowing shit: "Still reading it, Harold."

The fact is of course that he is a brilliant poet already: in his plays. A poet of incident and a poet in some of the longer speeches – what rhythm. My favourite is the 'slum slug' speech from *The Collection*[161]. I thought that last-gasp-wise this would frame my number 50. Lush is a vile word phonemically and in connotation. I recall seeing J. B. Priestley saying his taste in music had become for the lush – the way his old lips moved. I'm a shameful lover of lush right now.

---

[161] First performed May, 1961. The speech in question is by the old homosexual Harry and it takes place towards the end of the play.

50: Lush Life

Calm the measure, dear boy,
Life's just a royal road to gingham.
Suppress all fever, gambol-family on the beach
at Hastings.
Must cultivate the lush life.
Remarkably seek the lush life
per se,
tucked out of self.
Watch the gush of lush life
almost fervently contrived
in the town, but when lush life
opens fields it may-times falls foul,
dear boy, it's fright-en-ing.
Then there's Mae-Wan.
She is actually quite rancid in the pith:
full flop as lush.
She staggers well clear of the lush
sensibility, and she is a lush lout;
"Don't hold brief for lush louts
to the max", as our young mentor
says – she lolls over the laps
of male alphas, slave bangle as their fox.
She extracts meaty, sweating vignettes
ripe from the tongues of men, her babes
on her floors squeak about like
mavens; I tell a truth quite lightly to
crank my meaning up. Her days pass
by as all her visual brain is capsule-glued
to the ponkey mumbling tell-tale of eee
-mail. She won't turn a voodoo down.

29th December, 2007

This happened yesterday.
I had been bracing myself, of course, for something. I pottered out this morning with my pottering, pot-bellied, *harmless* shuffle to buy a *Guardian*; and there it was on the adjacent *Sun*:

Wedding Bells for Sab and Top Doc

A happy picture of them and the question in my mind: why do I care?

I went back to the flat and tore up the Guardian, when I saw it had also been (more demurely) reported there, seeing about me a chinzy over-stuffed tomb. I think I said before that I like to 'take disaster neat'. Like hell I do. Maybe Craigie did. Dunc don't. I paced the floor taking nips from her spirits bottles, but all that did was to stir up in me a raging thirst for oblivion. I had a cold lunch and the dregs of the red and went out, in the hope the wind would blow some sense into me, for a long walk. But the front was full of happy families so I headed inland to the dank narrow parts.

I ended up after some aimless circling at an anonymous boozer that fitted my mood. One step inside and the nostrils recoiled from the farty air. In the brown gloom I could not see a single woman drinker, while at the bar was a gaggle of beefy workers loudly joshing one another, with the josher-in-chief being a small but scary effort with a voice like a chain-saw.

The bitter proved to be undrinkable so I quickly ordered a *Guinness*. All I had to look at was my black drink and the half-drunk, half-dead inmates, as I had brought nothing to read. So I put some tracks on the juke box, which stubbornly kept playing *Je t'aime... moi non plus* to which Chain-Saw da da da dee dah-dah-dah-dah-ed along.

All of a sudden there was a burst of colour as about fifteen youths piled in (girls too) in red sports tops. They must have been a team using the community centre next door. How they debated what to have. And then, hot on their heals, came a bean-pole rasta and that very interesting and clever personality Detective Sergeant Keith Pavey. I thanked God the latter was hidden behind the former's hair and that they had chosen seats by the door. But there was no *escape*.

I would be visible to him at the bar so I sat tight and sipped the abandoned slimy bitter. Dare I ask one of the red-tops to get me a drink, pleading a leg problem? But I also needed a pee. I pee-ed. Ordered a *Guinness* and Jameson chaser at the bar and heard "Mr Poole. Over here!" The rasta was leaving and this was my date for the afternoon.

His lovely smile was missing, but not because of me. "Here, half of these little cunts are under age. I'll put out a PD67 [or something]." He spat into his mobile to get PCs round here "soon as you like" to ID all the red-tops "Bunging up the fucking bar." Then he relaxed.

"But getting to the bar is not really my problem as *you're* here. I'll have a pint of *Directors* and a double *Bells*... Oh, and the bangers and mash. Shake a leg, Bunter."

As we waited for the food he told me he'd heard "all about" me and Jenny. "Don't do badly for yourself, do you? And Welsh Peggy, too." He leaned forward: "But I want to make this crystal clear to you MISTER Poole. I intend to bleed you dry. And if you once refuse me what you have or what you can get from your love-blossom then it's your fuckin' DNA day. Capoosh?" Why no reference to his "mate" Modrick? "I don't know what you did, but you look like a paedo to me. Peggy says you were not much cop in the sack. Adds up, dunnit?"

This twinge of ego-wound made me bold: "I've heard enough. I'm off."

"No, you are not fuckin' *off*. You own me thirty quid, arse-features."

I gave him all I had on me (about £27) as the food arrived; after which I had to see him eat. I don't know what Pavey had in the way of teeth, but they were ineffectual. He re-mashed the mash and seemed to suck the sausages to pulp. But first, he laid the latter in his lake of ketchup stirring it up with the spuds and gravy – then forked it precariously into the gob. And then the master-stroke: he topped up with beer... talking, talking now (my track played at last [162]).

---

[162] See footnote 114 and associated text.

Yes, he talked and talked and talked, about anything that came into his head, as if rummaging for something – which he soon found. This was his 'girl' and this was sex *vis-à-vis* Crazy Pavey. The girl was Thai, and she had gone back to Thailand "for a few days to tie up a few loose ends." In fact he had not seen her since mid-November. Then, as if to bury that fact and to wipe the sceptical lights from my eyes, he piled on facts about all they did in bed, from how she should "throw her hair back" at hot moments, about the special things she wore for him; but mainly (Oh Christ!) about her "taste". I don't want to think of the mouth of him. Her taste was his heavy *motif*; and all articulated, all elaborated and coloured in, through the churning pub grub. Waxed lyrical – *smeared* lyrical.

"Look really..." I got up to leave.

I wonder if he had learned this in some course-module of copper-college, but quick as a rattle-snake he pincer-ed the ring finger of my left hand in the sharp nails of his right. He was very strong, and it hurt like hell. The force hardly waned and it was all I could do not to cry out. So I had to listen to more pornography. Actually that was what most of it was surely – his remembrances of DVDs past. Then (it seemed impossible) he *increased* the pressure, as he was suddenly angry that nobody had answered his call to do a mass-ID of the red-tops. "Useless shit-bags", he explained, before expanding on the "flexibility" of Teeranat. Then... "Ah! My colleagues." He stood up, and I ran for my life dripping red.

Back 'home' it was 1-4-1[163], then Sabbine's number. I had seen off a half bottle of vodka only a spot of which had been poured on my finger to disinfect it. The finger was now wrapped in a pair of Jenny's tiny knickers. I'll try to set down our conversation as accurately as I can.

Sabbine Stripentau: Hello?
Jack Craigie: It's me, Jack.
SS: [*pause*] What do you want? [*no hint of surprise*]
JC: I don't know... exactly.
SS: [*rapidly, overlapping me*] Your congretuations, I know it! [*silly laugh*]
JC: That bloody man is spiritual poison to you.
SS: But he did not kill any of my children. And that is what you say a plus of him. [*louder silly laugh*]
JC: I miss you.
SS: [*silence*]
JC: I don't know why I said that. But it is true.
SS: You contradict yourself somewhat.
JC: Look, I'm in pain here. Physical as well as mental, in fact.
SS: Your bad guilt from killing Nobby?
JC: From leaving you. For being ... like I was. For the whole thing really.
SS: [*more laughter, not silly*] Oh that's OK. I'm very heppy now. And Nobby... well, he was a problematical little boy. I forgiff you Jeck.
JC: I don't understand.
SS: Look, I discuss this with Berry, who is a very kind and subtle man. He knows many, as you call, *flexible* psychiatrists who can tell that you were under effort of mind. An

---

[163] This holds back the caller's number.

illness of personality. And, with mention of the drown-event, he did like to play divers with me for sure. Use what Berry calls your famaus imagination.
JC: What are you talking about?
SS: You understand you will only be locked away in some mild amenity for short years. They will have email in there. You can become one of my friends for sure.

31st December, 2007.

Fabulous[164]. Jenny has a CD of *South Pacific* – so *Some Enchanted Evening* can be the soundtrack to it. When I look over *Salthouse* bay from the bandstand, and the sun is sinking, I hear this song. That fixes the best of Clevedon for me. Fixes it in glowing magenta sunset, in a majestic cinema, with my mother, in 1954.

I will sit on the Salthouse beach in a niche I found yesterday in my little recce. There's only a handful of people about at sunset and whoever is about will see me as an eccentric and no more. I'm shielded from the road in any case.

My first thought[165] had been to pour the *Paddy* away. I have already finished all of Jenny's gin. But I took an executive decision to finish the *Paddy* (washed down with four *Mars Bars* just for old time's sake) reasoning thus: it will be painful so I'll need all the anaesthetic I can hold down. That said, in decanting the bleach into the *Paddy* bottle I splashed some on my hand and I felt drunk *and* in pain rather than any diminution of the pain. So, as she said "I contradict myself." Now my poor left hand doesn't know what's hit it. If this were a few days ago, this whole process would have inspired a Prynnish called *Inner Cleanliness* maybe based around his *Cool as a Mountain*

---

[164] In this, his final entry, Craigie's handwriting is very large and hyperlegible.

[165] Note the first line of his diary on May 30th.

Stream[166]. Or more likely it would be one of my silly-solipsist ones called *Some Decanted Evening*.
Some decanted evening... You'll become a gonner...

I suppose that what I am now is hyper-drunk – a higher level of drunk where everything is slowed down: each element is clear in the chain, but the links between the elements are mercury links; and you are not quite sure if it is you or somebody else initiating an action. "Higher level", I said? I didn't intend to get into the question of *why* in all this, but that's really it in the abstract. Jack Craigie never made it beyond the lowest level. What made him feel good or not was the whole of his world. A beautiful day was not significantly different from a delicious taste. Another's cruel action was equal to a grating noise or a clash of colours. And I used words like spitting out pips from fruit already savoured. Here are my 50 pip-patterns laydeezangents!

I at least have *intimations* now of the higher level and it breaks on my mind with the sentence 'The pain is moral necessity here'.

Bottoms up!

There before me on the table on which we ate the goose is a *Paddy* bottle of cloudy liquid, and I am sitting here in three pullovers and Jason's puffa coat. I'll put the bottle and the Walkman in a *Co-op* bag.

I can't breathe the air of myself any more.

---

[166] Both are advertising slogans from the early 1960s, the former for *Andrews' Liver Salts* and the latter for *Consulate* menthol cigarettes.

James Russell

The Gay Science[167]

And note his presence in the room,
  This customary single soul,
Reading and mouthing at the book.
  Do mark the scholar's scowl.
A pen's potential in his hand
twitches as a divining wand;
You'd think, attendant on this scene,
That solemn is the will to glean

The siltings from the best of thought
  Enfolded tight within these sheets
The formulae and mumbling art
  The sharp flesh and the sweet:
But no, this is a science gay
A source of swerves and disarray
Spreading quick blessings like seed corn;
He's Dada to the manor born.

His stern demeanour masks a mind
  More Edward Lear than Schopenhauer
Upon his hard disc you will find
  Some chocolate and a flower.
You see an aircraft through a cloud
Move slow, majestic, cold, and proud
But only when viewed from afar.
Inside it's flirting, drunk gloire.

---

[167] Almost certainly, Craigie did not intend this to be included in the collection. It only appears in pen and ink and it was un-numbered. The title is that of an essay by Nietzsche and the poem is identical in form to Wordsworth's *The Solitary Reaper*, a poem about which J. H. Prynne published a monograph in 2008.

But no-one quite knows why it is
   That he should read and write unceasing
And why his blue eyes ever quiz
   His diary's crabbed, blue writing.
He does not know and does not care:
The fact is that he's hardly there.
The words are all his pith and mass
They only think him as they pass.

Postscript

According to the police report, "a male pedestrian was seen to be walking in a very rapid but widely zig-zagging manner and was seen to frequently collide with oncoming pedestrians. Consequent on one such encounter, the male was seen to drop a carrier bag onto the pavement, its contents being smashed. Just before I apprehended him at 16.05, he was shouting at passers-by 'some enchanting evening', or words to that effect."

Craigie was arrested and very shortly after was charged with the murder of Norbert Stripentau. He confessed, and was quick to report his encounters with Keith Pavey. He also took some care to tell them where to find his concealed diary. He said, "It's all there and I don't want to go through it any more."

A week or so later, Craigie suffered a major stroke that impaired his speech and language comprehension. He could produce grammatical sentences but they were meaningless. Then, on the 29th of January he had a second and fatal stroke. There is some controversy surrounding the nature of his last words. Two of those present (Mrs. Anne McKewen and Mrs Jennifer Facey) insisted he had uttered the enigmatic but not meaningless *File bold. Hew through the weather*. However, one of those present (Mrs. Sabbine Ritter) was convinced she had heard, addressed to her, *I'll hold you to 'forever'*. It is two against one, and we must of course cleave to the principle of intersubjective truth (Palm and Hughes, 2007b).

www.ingramcontent.com/pod-product-compliance
Lightning Source LLC
Chambersburg PA
CBHW031314160426
43196CB00007B/530